HISTORY IN THE MAKING

CONTENTS

INTRODUCTION

If outstanding moments in sport are defined by drama and joy, then the first Irish Grand Slam win in 61 years will rank among the greatest of days in the country's illustrious sporting history.

For decades to come people will remember where they watched the thrilling finale to the Six Nations campaign in Cardiff.

The stepping stones to the Millennium Stadium showdown against Wales had been dramatic enough with narrow Croke Park wins over France and England and an edgy victory over Scotland at Murrayfield, but these games came nowhere near the nerve-shredding climax to the game in Cardiff.

Even the most imaginative script writer would have been hard-pressed to dream up such a heart-stopping conclusion as Ronan O'Gara kicked Ireland into the lead in the 78th minute only for a penalty to be conceded a minute later within range of the Irish posts. The rest is history as Stephen Jones missed by the narrowest of margins and a country erupted in celebration.

The ecstatic scenes in the stadium were matched throughout Ireland as a team that was in disarray 18 months earlier finally delivered on its rich promise.

This collection of outstanding reports, columns and photographs from the sports pages of The Irish Times captures the exhilarating journey on the road to Grand Slam glory. New insights are provided into how Declan Kidney restored the squad's confidence, built a team around Brian O'Driscoll and Paul O'Connell and created sporting history on a famous day in March.

The backroom team behind this publication deserve almost as many kudos as the writers and photographers. Kevin O'Hare, Michael Ruane and Paul Scott brought a huge level of expertise and enthusiasm to the book from the outset. Their skills were complemented by John O'Sullivan who also drove the project forward and never complained when asked to pore over the content for mistakes for the umpteenth time.

It would also be remiss not to mention Geraldine Kennedy, Maeve Donovan, Fran Walsh, Paul O'Neill, Carol Kirwan, Maeve O'Meara, Paul Farrell and Declan Murray for their encouragement and help.

MALACHY LOGAN,
SPORTS EDITOR.
THE IRISH TIMES

PUBLISHEB BY: THE IRISH TIMES LIMITED

EDITED BY: MALACHY LOGAN

IMAGES: THE IRISH TIMES STAFF PHOTOGRAPHERS: ALAN BETSON,
CYRIL BYRNE, ERIC LUKE & DARA MAC DONAILL
GETTY IMAGES

DESIGN & LAYOUT: KEVIN O'HARE & PAUL SCOTT

COLOUR REPRODUCTION: IRISH TIMES PREMEDIA

ISBN: 978-0-907011-34-7

THE MEETING

ENFIELD, CO. MEATH, DECEMBER

LAYING THE FOUNDATIONS
6:12:08, ENFIELD, CO.MEATH GERRYTHORNLEY

Speaking at the Greystones end of season annual dinner, Paul McNaughton was asked to discuss Ireland's Grand Slam. The Irish team manager began by stating that, in technical terms, this was the most efficient coaching squad ever to lead Ireland. It's hard to disagree. By this he meant there was more talent on this Irish coaching team than ever before.

In Gert Smal especially, the Irish management engineered quite a coup. The former Springboks number eight, who had coached the South African forwards to their 2007 World Cup win, had thrown his hat into the ring for the vacancy at Munster, created by Declan Kidney taking the Irish job. Although Kidney's highly regarded assistant at Munster, Tony McGahan, had been considered for a role on the Irish ticket, the Australian wanted to assume the top job at Munster for which he had always been earmarked. Smal, when sounded out for the position of Irish forwards coach, was receptive to the idea. The rest was up to Kidney and McNaughton.

Then there was Les Kiss, the outstanding defence coach in Super 14 with a CV the length of your arm, having worked with all the South African and several of the Australian franchises as well as the Springboks. Then there was the vastly experienced Alan Gaffney, adored by Leinster and Munster players alike after his time with both provinces, in addition to the re-hiring of Mark Tainton as kicking coach and the excellent Mervyn Murphy as video analyst. With Kidney's unique qualities as an organiser, planner, motivator and coach working alongside McNaughton, who was respected especially amongst the Leinster players he had managed, it made for quite a brains trust.

In essence, there were two strands to the Irish team's rejuvenation. The second was Kidney working his Midas touch most notably at the famed Enfield gathering in early December. But the first was assembling that coaching ticket. Ironically, the IRFU had turned in the first place somewhat reluctantly to Kidney. More than any other coach, he had helped kick-start a general rejuvenation in Irish rugby by transforming Munster from a team that took some notable Thomond Park scalps, but suffered heavily on the road (witness the 60-19 thrashing in Toulouse in November '96) to the undreamt of heights of a European Cup final in 2000.

In his last six Heineken Cup campaigns with Munster (2000-2002 and 2006-2008) he had coached his native province to two titles and four finals. In terms of winning pots and pans, Kidney had been, by some distance, the most successful coach in the history of Irish rugby. He had guided the Irish Under-19s to victory in the 1998 FIRA World Championship in France, won Triple Crowns and championships with Ireland A, the Ireland Schools and Under-19 teams, as well as promotion with Dolphin.

Yet it is far from clear whether the three-man IRFU Appointments' Committee of Noel Murphy, Pat Whelan and Neil Jackson, the same men who had misguidedly and prematurely awarded Eddie O'Sullivan another four-year extension in August '07, were even unanimous in their choice of Kidney. Nor will it ever be known how assiduously individuals such as former Leicester coach Pat Howard or former All Blacks coach John Mitchell had been sounded out. Both had coached in Ireland and were well connected to high-ranking IRFU officials.

But as Howard and Mitchell, the South African Heyneke Meyer and others ruled themselves out, and Munster marched remorselessly on to their second Heineken Cup success in 2008, so the media and public jumped aboard the Kidney bandwagon. With ringing endorsements from Warren Gatland, Matt Williams, McGahan and

DONNCHA O'CALLAGHAN GETS THE FIRST TOUCH

Michael Cheika, the IRFU had little choice but to appoint the Cork man.

Perhaps partly to absolve themselves of all blame were it to go wrong, as had happened with previous contrived marriages (Brian Ashton and Whelan, Gatland and O'Sullivan, O'Sullivan and Kidney) the decision was made – as with O'Sullivan in his later years – to give Kidney, correctly, carte blanche. He assembled the basic raw material of one of the best coaching panels in the world, something hitherto unthinkable for an Irish rugby team. So, while there was the Kidney factor itself, perhaps even a dollop of that hackneyed phrase "the luck of the Irish", and a dawning realisation amongst a so-called golden generation that their somewhat unfulfilled international careers were nearer the end than the beginning, the key ingredient was putting together a technically world class coaching team.

A fine flanker with Western Transvaal (1980-1983), Stellenbosch University (1984-1985), SA Gazelles (1984), SA Defence Forces (1986-1987), Western Province (1984-1993) and the Junior Springboks (1986), Smal would assuredly have represented the Springboks more than he did - playing against the touring New Zealand Cavaliers in 1986, a World Invitation XV in 1989 and in a Serge Blanco World XV team against France - but for the sporting boycott of South Africa's apartheid regime. He finished his playing days and initiated his coaching career with Rovigo in Italy, then coached the forwards at the Border Bulldogs, Western Province and the Stormers in the Super 12 from 2003 to 2005, reaching the 2004 semi-finals.

When Smal, who was keen to relocate to Europe rather than remain in South Africa, appeared on the radar, he was encouraged to apply for both the position of Irish forwards' coach and the Munster head coaching vacancy. Kidney met him first, and then, within three and two weeks respectively of their appointments, the coach and McNaughton spent a day with Smal in Cork toward the end of May. Almost immediately, he was identified as the first piece in the jigsaw. The three men talked at length about Smal's ideas on the game and what he would bring to the party. A deeply impressive man, with a wealth of knowledge on forward play and the game in general, Smal doesn't like to monopolise a conversation. He is not a ranter and raver, but is selective in raising his voice, and when he corrects players on the training ground he does so forcibly and to full effect.

Both in the Irish pack and even amongst the A forwards who were coached by him and the rest of the Kidney ticket in the successful Churchill Cup campaign during the summer, the players rave about Smal's technical ability, his attention to detail and his stature. Even the big players with the biggest reputations are slightly in awe of the big man named Smal. He, his wife Pattie and two children are happily ensconced in Dublin, where their eldest Dean is set to take the Leinster Schools Junior Cup by storm with Blackrock College. Paul O'Connell is such a noted Smal disciple that his teammates rib him about it. As John Hayes put it the week he played a record successive 48th championship game against England: "He's a World Cup winner as a coach, and obviously he's massive, physically, himself, so he commands respect. But just the way he talks, there's no messing with him. It's straight down to it. He knows what he wants and he gets his point across."

As a World Cup winner under contract up to the 2011 World Cup, Smal also has no compunction about aiming high with Ireland, and sees as the ultimate part of his job remit emulating the success he enjoyed with his native country. Ireland's lineout work, which for years had been the best in the world under Niall O'Donovan, was reborn. The Irish pack's pick and go drives were the foundation of some of the team's most compellingly sustained periods of pressure. Almost uniquely they reinvented the maul. A superbly well drilled unit, most notably in the build-up to Brian O'Driscoll's close range tries against England and Wales, you could have thrown a blanket over the pack.

Smal's analysis of the opposition, and his attention to detail in relation to lineouts and scrums, is relentless. So when, in the Grand Slam game, Stephen Jones sliced a touchfinder out on the full after the ball had been passed back into the 22, everybody knew what was going to happen next. This was their moment of destiny. They were trailing and had one play left to save the match and complete the Grand Slam. Rory Best had just come on as replacement hooker. Everybody in the ground and watching on television, not least the Welsh, probably knew he was going to throw to Paul O'Connell. Yet there wouldn't have been a shred of doubt within the team or amongst those watching, that Ireland's lineout would be as secure as Fort Knox. The rest was up to Ronan O'Gara, but the months of work on the training ground and through eight matches with Smal meant that the Irish outhalf would almost certainly have that opportunity.

Kidney received some sniping criticism for not taking over Ireland on their two match tour of New Zealand and Australia which followed just a week after Munster's Heineken Cup success, instead leaving Michael Bradley in charge as interim coach. But, along with McNaughton, Kidney wanted to make sure he had the coaching ticket right and combined a watching brief in the southern hemisphere with a recruitment drive. The pair interviewed a number of people in New Zealand and Australia, but the one person they wanted to meet, following on from their research, was Les Kiss. A former Australian Kangaroos rugby league winger and a member of the undefeated 1986 Australian team that toured Britain and France, Kiss had made a successful transition to rugby union in 2001 when he was recruited as the defence coach of South Africa. In the 2001 Tri-Nations championship, the Springboks had easily the best defensive record with the fewest tries (11) and the lowest number of points conceded.

The following year Kiss was given the opportunity to further expand his experience with three South African Super 12 teams - the Stormers, Cats and Bulls before returning to Australia in 2003, where he joined up as defence coach and video analyst with the NSW Waratahs. As is common with Australian coaches at the end of their domestic season, Kiss was on a month's coaching expedition to Japan when Kidney and McNaughton arrived in Australia, having returned to the IBM club he'd coached in 2003. Kidney and McNaughton rang the IRFU and requested that Kiss be flown business class on the long haul from Japan. In their round of interviews, Kiss's name had been mentioned in dispatches frequently as, statistically, the best defence coach in the southern hemisphere. He arrived in Melbourne the night before Ireland played Australia, and spent a day with the two Irishmen, before returning to Japan without even having time to watch the game.

The two couldn't have been more impressed. Aside from his track record, honed by then as much in rugby union as league, Kiss wasn't another of those tough-talking, northern English rugby league defensive coaches, à la Shaun Edwards, Phil Larder or Kiss's predecessors as Irish defence coaches, Mike Ford and Graham Steadman. Very personable and genuine, Kiss oozed enthusiasm from every pore. On returning home themselves, the Irish coach and manager informed the IRFU that they wanted Kiss, and to make him an offer. Kiss, in turn, contacted a few compatriots based in Ireland, such as the Leinster scrumhalf Chris Whitaker, who implored him to take the position, especially as he would never have encountered anything like the frenzied intensity and variety of the Six Nations. Kiss sorted out a job for his wife Julie and joined the Kidney team.

The Australian wrought something of a transformation in Ireland's defensive system. Under O'Sullivan, Ireland had developed a method designed to absorb pressure through phases without loss of shape or numbers. Kiss afforded greater adaptability and allowed the players more licence to think for themselves. Their line speed became much more aggressive and Irish defenders, or 'shooters', were allowed to leave the line in an attempt to envelop an opposition ball carrier, so stopping the move behind the gain line.

O'Sullivan had always been opposed to the concept of aggressive, so called blitz defences, even though some of the more successful sides, from Wasps to World Cup winners South Africa, employed the system. Kiss gives little away in his public utterances, but it quickly became clear that Ireland had abandoned the percentage, 'soakage' defensive system of before for a more aggressive defence designed to make things happen. O'Driscoll was particularly effective as a shooter - witness him picking off one of the two intercept tries which garnished the win in Rome. There were several other occasions when this tactic profited Ireland.

If there was a pivotal moment in the win over England at Croke Park it was O'Driscoll's close range try. This, in turn, could be traced to Jamie Heaslip's racing up to envelop Phil Vickery on 51 minutes. With a little help from the team's two unsung foot soldiers, Donncha O'Callaghan and Hayes, it was from the ensuing turnover that Stephen Ferris' offload and Luke Fitzgerald's handling skills helped to release O'Driscoll, who was blocked by Delon Armitage. Cue the penalty to the corner while O'Driscoll received treatment, and the ensuing scrum and pack power that led to the try.

Of course, it is a higher risk defensive system, and relies on trusting those inside to make their tackles and prevent offloads. Thus, when O'Driscoll shot up to cut off England's attack out wide and Andy Goode made the offload in Paddy Wallace's tackle to release Riki Flutey late on at Croke Park, the Irish captain was stranded beyond the ball and Flutey was away. Goode then had the vision to grubber through for Delon Armitage to outrun Marcus Horan and make the last minutes a good deal more fraught than they ought to have been, O'Gara, uncharacteristically, having left 11 points behind. But, in the main, the Kiss system has eminently more plusses than minuses.

The third important element of the new ticket was Gaffney. Ironically, McNaughton had been instrumental in lining up Gaffney for a return to Leinster from Saracens for the start of the 2008-09 season. The previous Christmas, 2007, he and Leinster chief executive Mick Dawson had sat down with Leinster coach Michael Cheika to broach the idea of having a senior figure alongside him, and had suggested Gaffney. There was considerable uncertainty at Saracens then, where Gaffney was head coach, and he was keen on a return to Ireland. McNaughton and Dawson met with Gaffney and by the end of March he agreed to come to Leinster as technical advisor/backs' coach. Now Ireland, however, were also looking for a backs' coach.

Far from opposing the idea, Cheika and Leinster were supportive of it. There was concern within the IRFU that Gaffney joining the Irish ticket might represent a conflict of interest. For example, how would, say, O'Gara feel about Gaffney coaching the Irish backs but also devising ways of stopping him and the Munster backs when wearing his Leinster hat. But, overall, the Australian's dual role came to be seen as an advantage.

On the way home from Australia, Kidney and McNaughton also met with Mark Tainton to confirm renewal of his position as Irish kicking coach. By and large, the ex-Bristol outhalf has a very good working relationship with O'Gara, allowing for the Irish outhalf's attention to detail, temperament and demand for precision, occasionally akin to that of a Formula One driver.

Pulling the strings masterfully was the head conductor, Kidney. In contrast to his predecessor, he was secure enough in his own skin to surround himself, and therefore challenge himself, with such expertise. He is, by nature, a careful man. While full of ideas, he will sound out trusted advisors before putting any of them into practice. Whether encouraged or discouraged, he still might pursue them, but he isn't averse to abandoning ideas on the advice of those closest to him.

AGE OLD FOES, IRELAND AND ARGENTINA GET TO GRIPS WITH ONE ANOTHER YET AGAIN

Kidney first conceived the notion of rotating his squad, or making three or four changes, for the Italy game in Rome, which came just a week after the win over France. Learning from the mistakes of the past, Kidney was determined to develop more of a squad culture, partly with the 2011 World Cup in mind, and reckoned that promoting the likes of Rory Best, Denis Leamy, Peter Stringer and Gordon D'Arcy not only wouldn't weaken the side, but would add a certain freshness as well. In the event, he was advised that such rotation for the Italian game would be premature. Taking that on board, he informed his coaching staff that he wouldn't make those changes yet and instead did so for the fourth game in Scotland.

From a coaching perspective, Kidney's job was to manage that dynamic, give all the coaches the right amount of individual airtime, take their ideas on board, put them all in the pot, stir it around and find a suitable interaction amongst the group.

Mervyn Murphy was also allowed to contribute at coaches' meetings. Always pasty white, from endless hours working in video dungeons, he will break down opposition games in piecemeal format. He detected that there was space behind the English lineout for a chip over the top by the scrumhalf, and, but for the angle of Tomas O'Leary's kick against England, the ploy might have yielded a try for Tommy Bowe. Murphy would hardly have been unique amongst video analysts in noting that, as in most defensive systems employed by Shaun Edwards, the Welsh pushed up hard and in, with the wingers compressing the line and therefore leaving space out wide for a deft cross kick.

On the training ground, Smal had the Irish forwards aware of what was on and how he wanted the scrum aligned, Kiss simulated the Welsh defensive system, using those players not on the starting team, and under the watchful eyes and instructions of Gaffney and Kidney, the Irish backs perfected this strategy. Helped by Gavin Henson having come on for the injured Lee Byrne at fullback, Bowe duly scored off O'Gara's crossfield chip in Cardiff.

All of this was a long, long way off the preceding August when the new management ticket first met up with an expanded Irish squad in Jury's Hotel in Cork, while, fittingly, training in Pres Cork. Kidney was taking them all back to his coaching roots. Aside from the players meeting Smal and Kiss for the first time, the coaching ticket was also introduced to the media and, almost immediately, a heightened sense of optimism was created by the sheer quality of that panel. With Kidney's renowned Midas touch, miracles were expected overnight. A week after a routine rout of the Canadians, highlighted by Keith Earls scoring at Thomond Park with his first touch in international rugby, some of us were guilty of believing Ireland could topple the All Blacks at Croke Park. This was ridiculous really.

The All Blacks were the reigning Tri-Nations champions and had won ten of their previous 12 matches in 2008. They arrived in Dublin on the back of a five game winning run, having beaten Australia (three times) and South Africa before their second string had accounted for Scotland by 32-6 in Murrayfield the week before. By contrast, Ireland had beaten nobody of note in a year, having won just six games from 14; at home to Italy twice, to Scotland and Canada as well as, barely, against Namibia and Georgia.

Furthermore, a new provincial coach might generate the same optimism going into the first round of the Heineken Cup in mid-October, but by that stage he would have had about 15 weeks of solid foundation work, including pre-season training, a couple of friendlies and five or six Magners League games. Kidney and co had had those five days in August, and a fortnight leading into the Canadian game before the week of the All Blacks match. That said Ireland performed badly, even by their own expectations.

They spent most of the 80 minutes hanging on for dear life, but showed little or no attacking verve save for a couple of breaks by Luke Fitzgerald in midfield. O'Gara had an especially poor game and, once Tommy Bowe was binned and a penalty try conceded on half-time, the game was up. To a desultory, muted capacity crowd at Croker, Ireland escaped somewhat lightly in losing only 22-3 as even the All Blacks became a little bored.

The new coaching ticket had been given little room for manoeuvre by the IRB decreeing that world rankings at the end of the November Test window would determine seedings for the 2011 World Cup in New Zealand. A further legacy of O'Sullivan's last year was that Ireland's ranking had slipped to eighth, leaving them clinging on to the final second tier seeding. Unless Ireland beat their old bugbears Argentina, they would drop to ninth, below the Scots, who had nearly beaten South Africa while Ireland were labouring against New Zealand. This World Cup seeding scenario assumed a near manic importance as it made the Argentina game simply a must-win.

With Juan Martin Hernandez aggravating a hamstring in the warmup and joining Felipe Contepomi on the sidelines, the below strength Pumas were forced to replace him with a 22-year-old debutant Santiago Fernandez. When he stepped up to address his first penalty and steered it wide, one knew immediately that they were likely to score only three or six points even if they'd been there until midnight. In the pantheon of sometimes taut, but often dreary, arm wrestles between these two increasingly bitter rivals, this was right up there. By all accounts, the post dinner standoffs and drinking challenges were more entertaining than the match.

The Irish forwards did beat up the Argentinian pack, for which they received scant credit. Nonetheless, it was a horrible game to watch, and was probably a horrible game to play in. Ireland pulled more than a score clear only in the last five minutes, thanks to a fifth O'Gara three-pointer and a Tommy Bowe try off the outhalf's crossfield kick to win 19-3. That it took Ireland so long to wear the Pumas down can be attributed to the high stakes and the team's lack of confidence. Afterwards, the level of introspection by the management was high. The performances had been a shock to Kidney and the coaching team. It was agreed that if Ireland played like this for the next six months they'd be going nowhere fast. With the stinging criticism of George Hook on the RTE panel ringing in their ears, the players also took the performances badly. This was due partly to an unrealistic level of expectation, not just among the media and public but amongst the squad as well.

Against that back-drop the squad assembled in the Marriott Hotel in Enfield. They had previously often decamped to Lanzarote for warm weather training and some bonding, but many of them were sick of travelling abroad for a Christmas break. In a further example of the more relaxed regime, the management took the players' views on board and decided to stay in Ireland. The optimum solution was to find a base with a training ground on site so as to minimise the time spent on buses. Kidney and McNaughton checked out the Enfield Marriott, which boasts an excellent, all-sport training field known as a 'prunty' pitch. The under-20s had stayed in Enfield and so, too, had Sunderland in pre-season. Hence, if it was good enough for Roy Keane, well . . . Coming the week before Christmas, and straight after the demanding back-to-back third and fourth rounds of the Heineken Cup, there were so many walking wounded that little could have been achieved on the training ground anyway.

It was decided that they'd spend a lot of time talking amongst themselves, specifically about the game plan, so there were numerous discussions, first between Kidney, McNaughton and the senior players, then with the other coaches and senior players, before the squad was broken up into groups. Much has been made of the honesty that ensued, and especially Rob Kearney bravely raising the vexed question of the Munster/Leinster divide and whether the Munster players cared as much about playing for their country. Ideally, Kearney would probably have preferred this to remain in-house, but O'Gara revealed all in an interview with The Sunday Times.

The most important aspect, however, was to sit down and sort out how Ireland wanted to play. Despite limited time together before the Six Nations, there was a general consensus that Ireland had to work on the development of the game plan and arrive at a clear idea of that strategy between coaches and players. All were given their say, and marrying the various and often conflicting views of how Ireland should play was the toughest part of Kidney's job. O'Gara, for example, a devotee of McGahan's at Munster, wanted to run the ball more from all corners of the pitch. O'Connell wanted first to take on the opposition up front. What were Ireland's strengths? Their weaknesses? How best could they highlight the former and disguise the latter? The senior players had certain ideas, and so too the coaches.

No less than the IRFU, some of the players would have had reservations about Kidney's appointment. Many of them, especially the Munster players, had already been coached for many years by Kidney at Munster and, in some cases, even at school. O'Gara especially, had hardly made a secret of his admiration for McGahan in the previous year or so.

A player such as Donncha O'Callaghan, who likes his targets mapped out for him, would have remained an honourable supporter of O'Sullivan right up to the stale end of his tenure and beyond. Even O'Driscoll had experienced a slightly fraught parting of the ways with Kidney when the coach left Leinster and returned to

Munster after one season. Nor would he have enjoyed his captaincy being held up for scrutiny, where before under O'Sullivan, it would not have been questioned, though in truth, it probably did his form no harm.

Like the others though, even O'Callaghan will surely already be reflecting on possibly the most decorated playing career of any Irish rugby player - a Grand Slam, two Heineken Cups, three Triple Crowns, that Under-19 World Championship - and conclude that Kidney's Midas touch was instrumental in most of it. In any event, the general consensus amongst the players was that the time for a change had come.

Kidney himself likes his teams to establish territory as a bedrock of their game. It emerged that there had been confusion in the November internationals about the players' interpretation of Kidney's territorial game, the players judging this as a signal to kick everything from their own half. Kidney explained himself by stressing it was never the intention just to kick for territory. It was up to the players to make calls on that, so there was clarification on that issue. The manner in which Ireland went wide off a pre-called lineout inside their own half for the length of the pitch try by Jamie Heaslip in the opening Six Nations win against France was the clearest manifestation of that change in emphasis. Such a move simply wouldn't have been called in the more rigidly interpreted game plan of November.

The frank, no-holds barred discussion amongst senior players and coaches on the Tuesday morning helped clear the air. Kidney vowed that the coaches would take on board all the views expressed for the next two mornings and come up with a more clearly defined game plan to be presented to the entire squad before the players returned to their provinces. In the meantime, the entire squad was also broken up into workshops and another issue to emerge was the players' irritation and frustration with the standard of training pitches which Ireland had been forced to use. 'Okay, from now on you are going to train on top class pitches,' they were assured and after Christmas and during the Six Nations they trained at the RDS.

So Enfield was all about defining the direction of the play, marrying what the coaches wanted to do with what some players wanted to do, and Kidney's ability to come up with a coherent playing strategy. The second, more publicised aspect, was the raising of the supposed Munster/Leinster rift during a workshop led by O'Gara, or more specifically the concern expressed by Kearney about the passion of the Munster players for the green jersey. This was discussed for the guts of an hour and it was no harm that the subject, heretofore a monster that dare not be mentioned, was raised. "Fair play to Rob for doing that," recounts McNaughton. "It was a ballsy thing to bring it up. But that wasn't the reason we won the Grand Slam! You know what I mean? You've got to put it in perspective. Ireland didn't win the Grand Slam just because guys said 'actually I do ****ing want to play for Ireland'.

"I played for Ireland and I know that the Munster guys want to play for Ireland and I know that the thing was, if anything, when Ireland was going bad, and when your provinces are going well, sometimes you want to get back into your provinces because that's a good place to be and the Irish camp was a bad place to be if you were doing badly. So I can understand that dynamic but ultimately guys want to play for Ireland and the other big thing was, players know, despite the growth of the European Cup, despite the hype of the European Cup, despite the fact that it's a fantastic competition and there really are some intense, local battles, the standard generally, outside of a couple of matches, is not up to Test standard. Test standards are a step up. The players always knew this."

That being said, when Munster or Leinster travelled to Clermont and Toulouse in the last couple of seasons, they were encountering sides studded with high class foreign imports in teams that would easily be superior to France on many days. Likewise, the regular head-to-heads between Munster and Leinster wouldn't be far off Test standard either. For what it's worth though, the Munster players reasserted that, for all their two Heineken Cups and three Triple crowns, no less than their Leinster or Ulster teammates, they had all underachieved with Ireland. The Grand Slam was mentioned as a realistic target, if not that season then, because of the senior players' age profile, sooner rather than later.

Padraig Harrington was also brought in to talk to the entire squad on the Wednesday evening. The players hadn't been informed in advance, and having taken their seats, were taken aback by the presence of Ireland's three-time Major winner. For the best part of two hours Harrington spoke as candidly as he could about the way he approached golf, specifically the majors, and the way he leaves bad decisions or bad shots behind him and moves on. But what had particular resonance for the squad and primarily the senior players was his account of how he had transformed himself from a serial runner-up to a winner of three majors in two years. This the players could identify with. They were rapt, and inspired, in equal measure. He would have spoken for another hour if time had allowed. Afterwards, Harrington and the players shared a pizza and a coke. As these things go, it had been a memorable evening for them.

Before breaking up on the Thursday, the squad trained on the prunty pitch and gently went through an outline of the game plan devised by the coaches, with many of the injured players assuming a watching brief. Finally, the players were asked if they had a clearer understanding of the game plan and it was abundantly obvious that their understanding on leaving the camp was on a different plane from when they had joined it.

Off Kidney, Smal, Kiss and Gaffney went, meeting regularly for hours on end to go through match scenarios and harness the new game plan, whilst also attending provincial games as often as possible. By the time the squad assembled for the first camp, there was a much better mood generally, not least because Leinster and

SQUARING UP TO THE ALL BLACKS

Munster had qualified from their pools for the knock-out stages of the Heineken Cup.

The players could also see that, as promised, the new game plan had been worked on assiduously by Kidney and the coaches. Playing territory was still a key component of the plan. The advent of the Experimental Law Variations had made that a fait accompli. But now this could be achieved by moving the ball wide as much as by kicking it. As it was also felt that Ireland had a very good kicking game, this was now shared across the line, from Tomas O'Leary at scrumhalf, to O'Driscoll's right boot, Kearney's howitzer left boot et al.

Basically, it wasn't rocket science. It was about getting into the opposition's part of the pitch, being very patient, working hard and ensuring, as much as possible, that the minimum Ireland must extract from each sojourn upfield was a penalty. A new-found level of patience was critical. "Don't panic when you get to their line." "Don't run it for the sake of running it but when it's on, when the ball is quick and the defence has been stretched, go for it." They initiated various ways of moving it fast, out wide or going up the middle, but there was greater emphasis on taking the opposition on up front.

This may sound simple enough, and may not be diametrically opposed to most other game plans, but it was certainly more practicable than, say, the French game, and it was also more tactically flexible than before. Ireland played some of their most enterprising, attacking back play in the opener against the French and in the last game in Cardiff. But in between times they came up against a superb English defence which left them no option but to batter away closer in, while against the Scots they were under the cosh for large tracts of the match. A recurring theme in all five matches, which brought to mind many famous Munster wins in Europe - dating back to the Heineken Cup semi-final win over Toulouse on a sweltering hot April day in Bordeaux nine years before - was how Ireland cranked up their intensity to yield a crucial score, more often than not in the third quarter.

If there was one defining moment, it was in the third quarter against England at Croke Park around the 52 minute mark. With O'Driscoll down injured and receiving treatment after Delon Armitage's late tackle, his chief lieutenants, O'Connell and O'Gara used the time out to consider their options. In a low-scoring game - Ireland were leading 6-3 - most teams would have opted for the eminently kickable three-pointer. To a crescendo of approval, the Munster duo opted for the kick to the corner and O'Driscoll returned to the fray. One can only imagine what was going through the minds of some of the English players. 'Oh ****, they're going to the corner.' And Ireland weren't leaving without the try they sought.

There was no question of them not winning their own throw. Their lineout had been secure all day. John Hayes was nearly worked through a cleverly created opening. On and on they pummelled England, through scrums and close range drives. Everyone knew they would stay there until they scored, which O'Driscoll duly did almost five minutes after the decision to go to the corner. Such confidence, in themselves and each other, and such patience wouldn't have been within the team's remit, even as recently as the previous November. For the confidence, the patience and the absolute trust in one another had all emanated from the shock of a disheartening autumn. Out of little acorns and all that.

IRELAND v FRANCE

CROKE PARK, FEBRUARY

WE'LL DESTROY FRANCE AT LINEOUT AND SCRUM

6:02:09, CROKE PARK, **LIAM TOLAND**

AT LONG last the anti-depression tablet has finally arrived, a full Croke Park two weeks running! Tyrone and Dublin started the ball rolling nicely last week. Who would have thought that 164,600 recession-suffering people would fill the massive stadium within seven days? Where are all these people hiding when the drivetime gurus are killing us slowly?

I can't wait, strolling down Jones's Road amongst all the fellow sufferers but free from trouble and strife. Come On Ireland! If I'm prepared to fork out my last €90 and make a weekend of it then you might oblige me with a humdinger. And why not? As Rumpole of the Bailey was wont to comment, "I'm all alone and leaderless" and in many cases both French coach Marc Lievremont and indeed England supremo Martin Johnson must be feeling the heat of successful rugby careers followed quickly into the lonely slot of the "leader". But for Lievremont, tomorrow could be his Waterloo. Why?

At the risk of ignoring vast aspects of our opening fixture tomorrow I would simply like to focus on two areas of French weakness, the scrum and particularly, the lineout. In the former David Wallace is key. Not as the source of ball but the decoy destroyer. It's high time the 10 metres (when refereed) is exploited. Precious little has been developed over the months. Why not swap both Wallaces at scrum time? Paddy could pack down on the flank, out of harm's way, with David at 10 and Ronan O'Gara shoving out one. "I pity the poor fool," as Mr T was apt to say, that would take David Wallace down with a 10-metre head start. Over the months he's attacked within inches of space. He can exploit the French. And after he's destroyed the French inside backs and they're very worried, tired and sore use him as a decoy to unleash the back three.

There's no doubt in my mind that outhalf Lionel Beauxis will suffer from his time spent at fullback with Stade Français and both Florian Fritz and Yannick Jauzion will have to accommodate him defensively. On the 10 or so scrums Ireland have tomorrow they should launch Wallace into the French which would certainly upset the best laid plans of mice and men.

So to the lineout where the French are plainly out of their depth. At the risk of sounding clichéd, the "Caveman" Sebastien Chabal is as about as much use as a one-legged man in an arse-kicking competition or an ashtray on a motor bike. The lineout is what will win this match for Ireland. The French may have something barmy up their sleeve, but to come to Croke Park with Chabal in the secondrow is bonkers. In the upper reaches of the South stand in Thomond Park I tracked Chabal for minutes on end. That night Sale Sharks were demolished and he was brutal.

When Brent Cockbain finally arrived, coach Philippe Saint-Andre decided to replace the impressive lineout specialist Dean Schofield and persisted with Chabal. He is an enormous influence on any fixture when motivated, but, unlike soccer, you can't carry a player (especially in the secondrow) for 78 minutes expecting him to poach a goal at the death. Please do not be fooled by the cameo ball carry every 20 minutes; watch him in the interim. He does nothing.

JAMIE HEASLIP TAKES THE DIRECT ROUTE

What makes it all the more galling is their captain, Lionel Nallet, is no leaping salmon. He is a powerful player in the mould of Brad Thorn, but like the All Black he doesn't have the aerial powers to be the main option. To combat this, Ireland have four excellent options and must utilise their advantage by getting blindside wingers into the line causing as much confusion to an uncomfortable looking inside backline. Adding to French woes, Imanol Harinordoquy is included for his aerial prowess. But he, too, is lazy; a limelight player when the team is going forward but not so hot in the trenches.

The relevance of the Irish dominating both the scrum and lineout is paramount. Although second favourites for the Championship at 3 to 1 behind Wales, they are fourth in line to be the top tournament try scorer, behind Wales, England and France. This is a worry of which the bookies are also aware. Tomorrow Ireland need to utilise their far superior set-piece, but in particular the lineout. They will steal ball from the French and must focus in on tries when they do so. I genuinely can't wait to see Robert Kearney (if fit) in full flight, working off Brian O'Driscoll.

Speaking of Kearney, his opposite man tomorrow is right back in form. Clement Poitrenaud's performance in the rain in Bath last weekend was part Kearney and part Pat Murray (Munster and Shannon). He has certainly developed from the man who coughed up a try to Wasps' Rob Howley in the Heineken Cup final that got away. He is worth marking closely. Over the weekend don't forget the battle for the Lions number 10 slot. We'll have to include Brive's Andy Goode who becomes the sixth outhalf in eight English Tests, freeing up Danny Cipriani for the Saxons and the odd fashion show in Milan.

Tonight I wish the Ruddocks the very best in what will be a wonderful night for the family. An Irish mother Bernie, father Mike, the Welsh Grand Slam winning coach and their two sons Rhys and Ciarán, who start for Ireland in the Under 20 international against France in Athlone. Come on the Haddocks! Of course if this wasn't all too mad, you could cast an eye on Twickenham tomorrow and observe how Stade Français openside Mauro Bergamasco performs at scrumhalf for Italy against England. God help him!

NORTHERN PIECES FIT NICELY INTO THIS JIGSAW

7:02:09, CROKE PARK, **KEITH DUGGAN**

WHEN MATT Williams checked the teletext and saw Paddy Wallace's name on the Ireland team to face France this evening, he couldn't contain his joy. The Ulster coach is back in Australia for a couple of weeks, thus missing the heavy snowfalls across Belfast during the week. On the morning of the team announcement, Wallace identified the decision of Williams to install him as Ulster's regular inside centre as a key reason behind his elevation to the Irish team after a long and sometimes frustrating few seasons as an understudy.

Williams, though, was reluctant to overstate his input to Wallace's achievement, instead happily predicting how his man's new partnership with Brian O'Driscoll might work. "Paddy's ability and attitude were never in question and it was clear that he had the talent to go on and play at the elite level. He has worked hard and played so well to put himself in this position. And what I think and hope now is that Paddy can really give Brian O'Driscoll the space he needs to do his stuff. He brings so much to this position. You know, Brian O'Driscoll is there with the best centres in the world and some of the things that have been said and written about him in the past few seasons have been disgraceful. So I am really excited to see if playing alongside Paddy can just get him just that bit of space."

The immediate success of the central partnership may be critical to Ireland's well-being in this Six Nations. But the inclusion of Wallace and his Ulster teammate, Stephen Ferris, at number six is a handsome reflection of the welcome return to form for the province after several tumultuous seasons. It is apt that a decade after Ulster pioneered what has been a stunning trail of Irish provincial success in Europe that there should be a renewed buzz around Ravenhill again.

The parallels between playing within a strong and confident club structure and making an impact at international level cannot be overstated, as Ferris alluded to when he spoke after learning of his selection this week. "Definitely. When you are playing good rugby and with Ulster getting a few wins, it would have been really disappointing this time if I hadn't made the grade. Last year, Ulster were sitting at the bottom of the table and confidence was low in general so it wouldn't have felt as bad not getting picked. Matt has put a tremendous amount of work into me as a player and he has been an influence on me mentally. He has helped me get my head right. Before, I would have just gone out there running around with my hair on fire. He has got me to calm myself down and to think about my game. And I am really enjoying doing that."

Ferris seems to belong to the long Ulster tradition of producing huge yet seemingly gentle men who have the ability to wreak havoc on a rugby field. David Humphreys, Operations Director at Ulster, chuckles down the phone at this suggestion. "Well, I don't think any of us who know Stephen well would ever describe him as gentle. All I know is that when I was playing outhalf, it was great to see his name on the team-sheet because he is just such a powerful player and getting stronger all the time; he handles the ball well and is fantastic at creating space. And Ireland has been producing an incredibly high standard of backrow forwards for 10 years now that it is extremely hard to break into the Irish side. But I do genuinely feel that if Stephen gets a run of games that he can become one of our great backrow exponents."

Ferris will be the lone Ulster accent in what is largely a Munster pack wearing green. Ulster's famous Christmas victory down at Thomond Park gives him plenty of credit in terms of bragging rights, but as he grinningly admits: "As the only Ulsterman there, I keep quiet in case they gang up on me." But although he is joining a unit that train and play together week-in week-out, there is no sense he is crashing the party. "The Irish backrow is so competitive. Munster are playing good stuff and Ulster have stepped up their game, so it is a tough contest.

"David Wallace is probably playing the some of the best rugby he has played in his career. And to play alongside a guy like that is something to look forward to. As for myself, I think there are definitely improvements to my game that I can make. And being in an environment where I can learn from guys like David Wallace and Paul O'Connell who have that experience behind them will hopefully stand to me well.

"My lineout work will be one of the issues. I never really got much lineout done with Ulster over the last few years. It is only this year that I have

BROTHERS IN ARMS AT A PACKED AND EXPECTANT CROKE PARK AHEAD OF THE FRENCH MATCH

become involved a lot more and so, coming into the autumn, it began to feel as if I was a lineout option. Paulie and Donncha O'Callaghan and the rest of the guys have confidence in me now. And it is great to feel that. Just to get that bit of confidence in the lineout when you go in can really have advantages for the rest of your game."

It is easy to imagine that it must be slightly more difficult for the Ulstermen to fit into a jigsaw made primarily of Leinster and Munster pieces. Even though provincial loyalties melt away once players turn up for international assignments, there is no escaping the fact that recent Irish selections have been overwhelmingly dominated by Leinster and Munster representation and that, therefore, it may be tougher for the Ulster players to develop the same kind of intuition and empathy the players from the other two provinces have from playing together year-round.

"Well, it might seem that way, but I feel at the top level of the game that isn't so much of a factor," says David Humphreys. "These are players at the peak of their game with a common ambition to play for Ireland and for the team to do well. It doesn't take long to get settled. If you take Paddy, his experience of having played number 10 for Ulster and Ireland gives him a real appreciation of the demands of space and the pressure that the outhalf faces, and that gives us a great advantage. Paddy has always been a really versatile player, I remember him coming in at fullback for Ulster and doing well there, and then suffering setbacks with injury and moving to 10. But his form at 12 has been exceptional and that has been reflected in this selection."

The Magners League victory against Munster mattered deeply to the Ulster players as a true means of measuring the progress they have made this year. A terrific Heineken Cup win over Harlequins would follow, before they finally bowed out of Europe with a fine away performance against Stade Francais. Dealing with Munster in Ravenhill is one matter, but to win in Limerick in the manner they did was deeply gratifying. "I think that there was just that kind of buzz," Ferris recalls. "You get it before games sometimes. The changing room went really quiet and there was just something about the day that we felt it might happen.

"And in fairness, if you threw the ball between a Munster player and one of us, it would have bounced for us. It was one of those days and you have to enjoy them. I definitely could have played better - I slipped off a few tackles. But I am always hard on myself. I always want to improve. And it was a good marker to lay down against a good Munster team."

Williams sighs for a moment when asked about that game, as he holds an ambivalent attitude. "It was an extraordinary night, yeah. But it was also just another game, mate. Whether it had a big influence on the boys, well, that is for them to say. I enjoyed it; it was an entertaining game and one that I will never forget. But the thing is, when we go back down there to play them again, we have to try and do the same thing. We went out a couple of weeks later to Stade with a bunch of kids and played brilliantly, so we just have to keep going every week. And the same holds true for the boys within the Ireland set-up, whether they are playing France or England."

That has certainly been Ferris's attitude: he quietly but firmly brushed off the suggestion that his name might be on the long list for the Lions tour. "I just think about the next game. Right now, that is France. You can have a loss of form or an injury so there is just no point in thinking too far ahead." He beams at the mention of Sebastian Chabal and concedes that his mother is a Chabal fanatic. "I just hope she will be cheering for me the next day. He is just one of these characters that always seem to be there on the pitch. It is just his look and his appearance that could put many a player off. But the Munster lads know him from Sale and I do think everyone is confident going in on Saturday."

This is the thing. February optimism is high and Ireland have already been tipped as likely Grand Slam contenders in several quarters. For Ulster fans, the input of the local boys will be critical, with Ferris seeking to impose himself in the loose and Paddy Wallace taking on an intriguing role. David Humphreys spent Thursday snowed in but intends to be in Croke Park this evening, while in Australia, Matt Williams will be up in the middle of the night to watch the broadcast.

The Australian admitted: "I wouldn't miss it for the world. One of the great joys of your life is seeing players that you believe in being rewarded, and so to see Paddy running out the next day is going to be special. And to see Paddy and Stephen there for the anthems, and maybe to see big Tom Court coming off the bench late in the game, will be one of the great joys of my coaching career."

IRISH AMBITION, DISCIPLINE AND DEFENCE IN PERFECT HARMONY

09:02:09, CROKE PARK, **GERRY THORNLEY**

IRELAND 30 FRANCE 21

IT'S ONLY one game, it's only a start, there are four games to go and the performance was not without its imperfections. Yet given the quality of the French display, this was a stunning opening to the championship for Ireland and could represent a landmark win. As a game, it was probably the best so far at Croke Park. Sure, the rout of England two years ago was the day of days and, in its sheer scale and sense of occasion, would take some beating. But as a contest, this surpassed even that encounter. You couldn't take your eyes off it.

For France turned up, no doubt about it. Indeed, let's be honest about it: in a wonderfully fluid contest which ebbed and flowed throughout, until Ireland put the game to bed with about two minutes to go, there were plenty of spells when France had the upper hand and looked set to continue their dominance of this fixture. Rediscovering the spirit of French rugby, Les Bleus rarely looked ruffled and were quickly into their adventurous stride. Admittedly they were often invited to do so by Ireland's kicking, but the ever-menacing Maxime Medard and his Toulouse kindred spirit Clement Poitrenaud counterattacked freely, in tandem with Julien Malzieu, and all their teammates were in the mood.

Ireland couldn't drop their guard for a second. A quick throw by Medard infield to Poitrenaud and one of several Sebastien Chabal rumbles set the tone and had the French fans in full voice. There was an inevitability about them drawing first blood with a wonderful, sweeping score, instigated by Florian Fritz crashing through Ronan O'Gara, given menace by Medard's deft chip up the touchline, Fulgence Ouedraogo's gather and link with Yannick Jauzion and finished off by Imanol Harinordoquy after perfect passes by Chabal and Malzieu. No doubt Les Kiss will find some flaws in the Irish defending, but most teams would have struggled to prevent that try.

Ultimately, there were many factors in Ireland's ability to respond then and to other moments of potential crisis, primarily their ambition and clinical finishing. The setpieces were excellent. John Hayes and co locked the scrum impressively for Jamie Heaslip to charge impressively off the base at the soft Lionel Beauxis channel. The quality of their lineout ball - Jerry Flannery's accuracy and Paul O'Connell masterful in the air - was significantly better. Tellingly, all three tries emanated from Irish lineouts, the first two with moves that could have come straight off the training ground.

Ireland's defending was top class, especially when scrambling back after French line breaks, epitomised by Tommy Bowe catching Chabal from behind after his searing burst before half-time. In the final analysis, too, Irish handling was more precise, and France let Ireland off the hook on a number of occasions with some surprising handling errors: you think of Thierry Dusautoir's knock on from the recycle after that Chabal rumble. But just as critical was their discipline when set against that of les bleus. As significant as any of the 10 penalties France conceded were the ones against Dimitri Szarzewski for going to ground straight after that first try, allowing O'Gara to post a second three-pointer, and Cedric Heymans not releasing for the match clinching penalty.

The French will feel aggrieved at the 10-2 penalty count (they did have three indirect frees as well), and at having to wait 76 minutes for their first full penalty. Munster and Leinster have been on the wrong end of most penalty counts when Mr Owens has been in charge, but they did benefit from their familiarity with his style, particularly his severity with players not releasing or going off their feet in the tackle. In this, too, as coach Marc Lievremont repeatedly acknowledged while masking his sense of grievance, the French were authors of the downfall. At times they looked like they could have been in a swimming competition.

To put this stunning win in perspective, not alone did it end a run of seven straight losses against Ireland's bete noir and represent a fourth win in

EYES FORWARD THE IRISH PACK PREPARE TO ENGAGE.

the last 27 meetings, it was their biggest win in the fixture since 1975 and the first time in 100 years Ireland have scored three tries at home against France. Ye Gods.

And the Six Nations will do well to throw up five tries in one match as good as those last Saturday and, just like that brace by France, nothing underlined the quality of this performance more than those three Irish tries. When Bowe came from deep behind a decoy shield off a shortened lineout, at last we had the all too rare sight of the outstanding Rob Kearney hitting the line, and his offload and Bowe's support run gave the move the impetus from which Heaslip made his stunning finish through the middle. That was the high point of a wondrous display by the number eight, but there were many big plays, right up to when he earned the last penalty after Luke Fitzgerald put in a flying tackle on Heymans.

The flaw in Ireland's performance was undoubtedly their kicking, but to O'Gara's immense credit he took the ball to the line and distributed superbly, in particular when Brian O'Driscoll steamed onto his pass to beat Beauxis on the outside and step inside Malzieu. He's been waiting for a pass like that with Leinster for some time. It was vintage O'Driscoll, and the high point of a superb all-round performance, punctuated by as fine a display of outside centre defending as this ground will see.

Credit to his leadership, too, after France countered the length of the field for Medard's try and a second Beauxis drop goal to put the game back into the melting pot, when he took on the responsibility to drill a raking touchfinder. It was from that kick that Heaslip's pressure on Beauxis and the pack's rumbling led to Gordon D'Arcy exorcising the pain of almost a year's absence to score with that remarkable footwork and strength of his. You could hardly have scripted it. That just made the feel good factor even better.

PRIVILEGE TO WITNESS EIGHT SECONDS OF MAGIC

09:02:09, CROKE PARK, **LIAM TOLAND**

EIGHT SECONDS is all it took for this group of Irish players to display to the world what we know they're capable of. Eight short seconds where five Irish players with 266 international caps between them could bring a nation to its feet to witness pure magic. What makes our game so unique is the components required to get the ball from Jerry Flannery on the touchline into Brian O'Driscoll's hands for a try.

In the 42nd minute Ireland had a lineout in the French half and Flannery stood in the loneliest of places. Start the clock. He released the perfect ball to Paul O'Connell at full stretch (one second). O'Connell then delivered the ball to Tomás O'Leary who hit Ronan O'Gara, wide and flat (three seconds). O'Gara's pass had 88 caps of experience built into it that allowed O'Driscoll a chance and four seconds later he touched down. To achieve this so many components had to click and it only took eight seconds!

I couldn't help but ask myself where were Sebastien Chabal and Imanol Harinordoquy, Lionel Beauxis, Florian Fritz and co when Ireland produced the perfect execution of skill and precision at such pace. When Ireland put pace on their play then even this outstanding French team struggled. I drew some comfort with this score as the aforementioned French players were having big games! But I still maintain that French selection with Chabal is flawed. When he carried, four times, he was immense but each carry lasted only 10 seconds. That's a total input of 40 seconds which leaves 79 minutes and 20 seconds. What else did he do?

However, his number eight colleague, Harinordoquy, was right up there with Jamie Heaslip as the performance of the day. Harinordoquy is a phenomenal athlete whose one handed take in the lineout was sublime. O'Driscoll's try is relevant because 23 minutes earlier Heaslip broke from a struggling Irish scrum in midfield and made huge ground towards Hill 16. A terrible pass to Rob Kearney ensued and the French stole the ball. This passage of play also took eight seconds but lacked the precision that followed. And, as I scroll through my notes from the match, there are vast periods where we struggled to keep pace with the French and but for French indiscipline at the breakdown in particular things could have been much worse at half-time. So to be up at half-time and win by nine points against opposition of this calibre was a serious beating.

Ironically Ireland's tries came from three Leinster players who were struggling for form for one reason or another and simply couldn't buy a try even if they tried! Then like buses three come along. All three are very much in the Lions race. Of the rejuvenated D'Arcy, what must Greystones centre Conor Cleary, way down in the second division of the AIL, be thinking? Two weeks running D'Arcy scores tries. The first was for Lansdowne FC, marking Cleary and then the second against Yannick Jauzion. Twelve months of patience and, of course, an awful lot of leg weights powered D'Arcy over the line yesterday.

Another power player is Rob Kearney. By the 11th minute he had made a hat-trick of catches all from kick-offs; the third being his best. He continues to be enormously ambitious on returning to terra firma, where he explodes forward not accepting his fate. In order to stamp his Lions Test place he could add a very offensive defence.

In the middle of all this we must look at areas for improvement! Ireland's kicking game was far too long and allowed a French back three to counter at ease which is exhausting for those charged with defending the strong runners. We subsequently out-tackled the French 95-71, but missed considerably more at 14 to five. All told, the Irish defence did incredibly well to survive the French running, which is at its best in the five-metre area through traffic. Tellingly RTÉ's build-up to the match showed the French in their state-of-the-art training ground.

And for those who saw it they may have noticed the drill the French were executing. All based on a 25-metre squared area where the ball carrier must get past a defender, pulling him one way in order to create space for the support runner. This they were able to replicate with ease throughout the game.

Secondly, Ireland need to increase speed on the ball from dead rucks. D'Arcy's try came from the Irish forwards bravely pummelling the French close in. But further out we need starter moves and this is where big ball carriers like Paul O'Connell can come in. His circle pass that resulted in Heaslip's try displays the advantage of offloading to a better placed player whose eyes are up and who is running hard. David Wallace, too, has more to offer from play. His dummy offload played a huge part in that first try.

So to next Sunday's selection. Paddy Wallace is a player with a specific skill set, where he can control, kick and pass but doesn't possess so much bosh. Therefore Kidney's selection at 12 must hinge on its role. As Ireland focused on slow ruck play, it prevented a more consistent flow of ball to 12 hence neutering Wallace to some extent. He was prevented from alternating between 10 and 12 and adding his influence. But next week he could be very valuable against the Italians in order to unhinge a stiff and aggressive defence.

Finally, the Lions watch! To the obvious contenders you can now add Jamie Heaslip. Fantastic.

LONG JOURNEY BACK GOES LIKE A DREAM

09:02:09, CROKE PARK, GAVIN CUMMISKEY

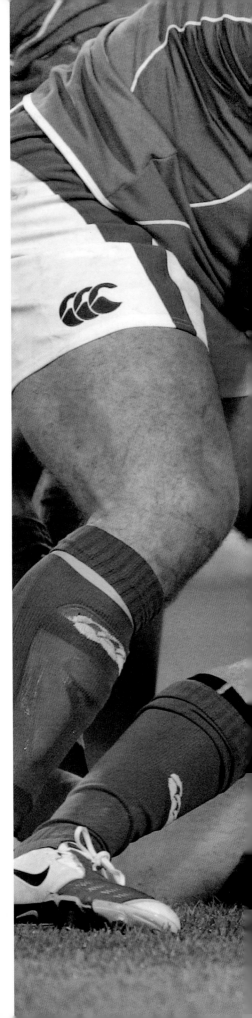

VAN MORRISON's 'Days Like This,' said it best. Another one of those memorable days at Croke Park when those in attendance realised they were witnessing something special and hopefully lasting. For sure, the French will be happy to see the back of north Dublin. The player reaction to Jamie Heaslip's try bordered on euphoric but too early in the match (36 minutes) for anyone to lose their composure. When Brian O'Driscoll swerved inside Julien Malzieu for a try with shades of his individual effort on the 2001 Lions Tour in Australia, he was immediately surrounded by the younger three-quarters who grew up watching their captain cut a swathe through world rugby.

Then came the remarkable, and for a time unlikely, return of Gordon D'Arcy. This has been a ridiculously undulating career with the highs now far exceeding the troughs. And yet, since D'Arcy suffered a complicated arm fracture against Italy in last season's Six Nations match he has undergone a nightmare recuperation period that included three operations. Last week he togged out for Lansdowne in an AIL Division Two fixture against Greystones. That was just to get some extra game time under his belt, having been unable to dislodge any three-quarters at Leinster since returning over the Christmas period.

Since first coming to prominence as a serious attacking talent during Clongowes Wood College's run to the 1997 Leinster Schools Senior Cup Final, D'Arcy has always been marked down for a long, fruitful career. Saturday's cameo role was evidence of this becoming a reality. Paddy Wallace may retain the inside centre berth for Rome but after the Ulster player eventually succumbed to a head wound, suddenly D'Arcy was back on the main stage. Within five minutes he found himself 10 yards from the French line, screaming for ball off Tomás O'Leary. The Corkman (seems like he has been there for years, doesn't it?) duly obliged.

"We'd done a bit of work on them and we knew in the 22 the forwards could carry, carry and we might be able to suck them in. I managed to get a one on one with a forward," said D'Arcy. Not just any forward but the usually impregnable grip of Thierry Dusautoir, who was unable to deny the Wexford native twisting over for a fifth Test-match try. He let out a deep roar as Jamie Heaslip, Rob Kearney and Brian O'Driscoll mobbed their rejuvenated friend. The realisation set in that France were groggy, on the ropes and Gordon D'Arcy was back doing what he does best - breaking the gain line.

The obvious line of questioning for the man who turns 29 on Tuesday was the long road back to fitness, especially considering Chinese whispers had him on the scrapheap just a few months back. Eleven months. Operation after operation and things didn't knit. Did you think that was it sometimes? "I'm back playing rugby now so I'm pretty happy," he says. How satisfying is that considering what you had to get through to get back on the pitch today? "Deccie (Kidney) has put a lot on the line by putting me on the bench, not having played a lot of rugby in the last 12 months. I played for Lansdowne last week. It was a big gamble on his part so it was just nice to be able to repay a couple

TRY SCORER JAMIE HEASLIP IS ABOUT TO BE MOBBED

of people who put a bit of faith in me."

He fended off any more queries trying to turn the situation into a romantic return to arms. It's simply not his way. D'Arcy is the type of fellow you would see at the back of the stands supporting Leinster when injured. The type of player who doesn't tog out for his club for personal reasons but actually buys into the promotion battle Lansdowne are currently embroiled in (they went top after a 25-5 defeat of Greystones with D'Arcy claiming a try).

Club rugby in Ireland is considered another sport by many professional coaches. Releasing a player is rare and a constant struggle so for an international, a Lion even, to feature was a huge boost to the bottom strata of Irish rugby; on life support since the advent of professionalism. "It just popped up. I decided it was a good idea because I hadn't played too much. You can make what you want out of a game like that. You can go and sit on the wings and do nothing. I got stuck into it and got as many touches of the ball as I could," said D'Arcy.

"I'd know a lot of the players, one of my friends is coaching and there are ex-Leinster players. The great thing is in a team like that they are playing for promotion so every game actually means everything to them. They were happy that I came in and didn't act the mick and got stuck into it and wanted to win the game as much as they did," he adds.

Lansdowne will struggle to regain his services for the rest of the season as an intriguing debate about the number 12 jersey begins. "When you come back from an injury you get a chance. Rugby is all about chances. Whether you take them or let them pass you by. Look back 12 months, Rob Kearney took his chance and look at the player we have now. I can only take the chances that are given in front of me," concludes D'Arcy.

O'DRISCOLL IS NOT GETTING CARRIED AWAY

09:02:09, CROKE PARK, **JOHNNY WATTERSON**

CALL IT maturity. Call it Declan Kidney's natural disposition. Call it Brian O'Driscoll's experience of career ups and downs, heightened expectations and, occasionally, crushed dreams. A win over France opened possibilities for this Six Nations Championship but few below in the stands after the Croke Park match were reaching for heroic imagery or promising Grand Slam crusades. "One game win momentum," said captain O'Driscoll summing it up somewhat frankly. No more, no less.

"Granted France are top class opposition. But at the same time let's not get carried away," he cautioned. You can't win a Six Nations with a first win but essentially you can lose it. We are where we want to be. We've played one game. We've won one game. We're happy with the performance. We'll enjoy it for a few hours tonight and then get on with Italy tomorrow. Simple as that."

Kidney's mood, or the one presented for public consumption, was equally dampened. His great capacity is to play down important wins even more than excusing defeat. The psychologist inside rarely stops intruding. Gracious to his team for their commitment and pluck when it was needed, he also found worth in the experience pool of the squad. Input even came from players who did not make the pitch.

"The lads have been great in the way they have been coming up with ideas," said the coach. "Strings (Peter Stringer) inside in the dressingroom, was putting in his tuppence worth at half-time. When you have that kind of experience there, it is prudent to tap into it and get fellas to come out with it. So it's their game plan. But it is still like 24 hours ago. We still have four teams (to play) and we still have to work really hard. If you've followed them (players) around for the last month you will have seen how hard they have worked. They should be extremely proud of themselves."

Closing down the French and extinguishing their confidence fuelled flair was also an important part of the winning narrative. Strangling their ambitious running game, imposing an Irish shape on the game was the winning of it. "Our defence was top class," added Kidney. "The forwards were immense. It's only right to mention Paul's (O'Connell) contribution during the week. He was brilliant. We are lucky that we have a great bunch of team leaders, the two lads here (O'Driscoll and O'Gara) and Paul. That aspect needed to be right today.

"If you give France free space they are brilliant. Some of the movements they were coming up with today were exceptionally good. A few times in the first half, when they were fresh, they made inroads on us. But we managed to close them off and no more so than in the last 30 seconds . . . the try wouldn't have affected the result but the boys had great pride in it."

An O'Driscoll try, replete with side step, highlighted some of the nonsense about him being a fading light, while his soldiering partner for so long, Gordon D'Arcy, sought to make a claim for starting recognition. It was trademark D'Arcy. A change of direction, a spin and natural strength took him over despite being festooned with French cover. "Gordon is a top-class international," said Kidney. "He asked me himself what I wanted him to do. I just asked him to play. He'll be clamouring for his place but Paddy (Wallace) did exceptionally well too."

And then there's Rob Kearney, Luke Fitzgerald, Jerry Flannery, Jamie Heaslip. A terrific win but Kidney and O'Driscoll remain shrewdly cautious. Baby steps indeed.

FRENCH NUMBER EIGHT IMANOL HARINORDOQUY AT HIS ATHLETIC BEST

IRELAND'S FORWARDS PASS PHYSICAL EXAMINATION

09:02:09, CROKE PARK, JOHN O'SULLIVAN

THE BODY language and verbal expression of players in pivotal, potentially game-defining moments can offer a mirror to the soul of a team. On Saturday at Croke Park the enthusiasm and commitment of the Ireland players was palpable from the stands. It wasn't simply apparent in the explosion of bear-hugging and backslapping that accompanied the three tries but the approbation dispensed for grittier contributions. There were numerous examples as when a jaded Jamie Heaslip was congratulated by a host of teammates after forcing French replacement wing Cedric Heymans to concede a late penalty, one that ensured there would be no nasty surprises in the final throes of the contest.

There is a vitality to this Irish team that has accompanied the new coaching regime but there is also an air of confidence. In times past Ireland might well have buckled when France cut loose but they didn't, hanging on, scrambling and then embellishing those virtues with tries. Experience would have helped when times were fraught on Saturday but there appears more than that, a commonality of purpose between management and players that is appreciated by all.

Nursing his usual quota of facial discolorations, Ireland second row Donncha O'Callaghan touched on the subject when he spoke about how much further down the road the Irish team now is under the new management. "I feel that player wise there is great clarity in our game-plan now. We know exactly what we're about. That's not making excuses for poor performances in the autumn (November Tests). We know what Les (Kiss) wants in defence; we know what Gert (Smal) wants in the forward play, (and) the way Declan (Kidney) wants us to play. There would have been little grey areas there in the autumn internationals but now there is pure clarity. You know when we hit the wide channels what we are trying to do, when we hit midfield, the same. Of course it takes a bit of time to bed in with the coaches. Like I said I'm not trying to look for excuses with regard to past performances but that extra time has been important."

The Munster secondrow confirmed that the players had spoken in the buildup about the importance of work-rate and commitment; about getting up and making that extra tackle, that clear-out or simply being there to support the ballcarrier. No one shirked their responsibility under the watchful eye of scrumhalf Tomás O'Leary, who chivvied and directed with authority. O'Callaghan smiled: "There was a great feeling among the team. There was a real will to get off the ground after you made your hit, get back up on your feet and make another tackle. I think Tomás (O'Leary) bullied the forwards brilliantly, shouting and roaring at fellas. That's all we need a bit of direction. He gave that to us. That's priceless. When you can get the likes of Stephen Ferris, Haysie (John Hayes) and Jerry (Flannery) screaming at you to get off the ground, you wouldn't be long there (on the ground). We have a saying, 'no logs lying on the ground.' You just heard fellas shouting that today."

The match was played not only at a breathtaking intensity but a breakneck speed that seriously examined player fitness. The age old argument about the comparison between provincial and international fare surfaced. O'Callaghan's answer brooked no argument: "International rugby is played at a different pace. "You just cannot afford to make any mistakes. The intensity of it is through the roof. You can't compare it to anything you play with your clubs or your provinces. It's a massive step up. You look around our dressing room and fellas were sucking after it (the game). I think we'll be all the better for that (experience) because it gets you up to speed for the challenges that you face ahead in this tournament. The breakdown was incredible. Maybe it is because you are playing against the best players but nothing is taken for granted. Every hit you feel it, every time in contact it's massive."

It was a theme picked up by Ireland's openside David Wallace. "Not only did they play with their typical flamboyance but they were physical and aggressive. It was a very hard fought game. They played well and that probably makes the victory all the sweeter. The pace of the game was very high. Any time we kicked it they ran it back, took quick throws-in and it can be very hard to play against because they are the best in the world when it comes to that. We tightened it up a bit in the second half and didn't give them as much space. It was still difficult as they were liable to score tries from anywhere."

Wallace was perfectly placed to analyse the performance of his backrow colleague Jamie Heaslip, a deserving winner of the man of the match accolade. "Jamie was brilliant; (he) left nothing for the rest of us. When he wasn't scoring tries he was poaching ball: he was on fire today. I had a quiet game myself in terms of attack but Jamie was brilliant, really potent."

The Munster flanker also explained the significance of the delighted melee that surrounded Gordon D'Arcy when he crossed for Ireland's third try. "Everyone felt for him when he was having the trouble (with his arm). Like himself, we were worried that he'd never get back here. That cameo, to come on and score a try was brilliant. Everyone was chuffed for him."

Italy next Sunday in Rome will provide a completely different assignment. On Saturday's evidence though, they will face an Ireland team that looks very comfortable in their own skin.

IRELAND 30-21 FRANCE

O'Gara pen	2:16	
	15:41	Harinordoquy try
	16:46	Beauxis con
O'Gara pen	18:32	
Heaslip try	36:35	
O'Gara con	37:41	
	45:14	Beauxis drop goal
	H-T	
O'Driscoll try	2:48	
O'Gara con	3:45	
	10:50	Medard try
	14:13	Beauxis drop goal
D'Arcy try	28:37	
O'Gara con	29:31	
	41:07	Beauxis pen
O'Gara pen	42:38	

IRELAND

- 15 **ROB KEARNEY** (Leinster)
- 14 **TOMMY BOWE** (Ospreys)
- 13 **BRIAN O'DRISCOLL** (Leinster, capt)
- 12 **PADDY WALLACE** (Ulster)
- 11 **LUKE FITZGERALD** (Leinster)
- 10 **RONAN O'GARA** (Munster)
- 9 **TOMÁS O'LEARY** (Munster)
- 1 **MARCUS HORAN** (Munster)
- 2 **JERRY FLANNERY** (Munster)
- 3 **JOHN HAYES** (Munster)
- 4 **DONNCHA O'CALLAGHAN** (Munster)
- 5 **PAUL O'CONNELL** (Munster)
- 6 **STEPHEN FERRIS** (Ulster)
- 7 **DAVID WALLACE** (Munster)
- 8 **JAMIE HEASLIP** (Leinster)

FRANCE

- **CLEMENT POITRENAUD** (Toulouse) 15
- **JULIEN MALZIEU** (Clermont Auvergne) 14
- **FLORIAN FRITZ** (Toulouse) 13
- **YANNICK JAUZION** (Toulouse) 12
- **MAXIME MEDARD** (Toulouse) 11
- **LIONEL BEAUXIS** (Stade Francais) 10
- **SEBASTIEN TILLOUS-BORDE** (Castres) 9
- **LIONEL FAURE** (Sale) 1
- **DIMITRI SZARZEWSKI** (Stade Francais) 2
- **BENOIT LECOULS** (Toulouse) 3
- **SEBASTIEN CHABAL** (Sale) 4
- **LIONEL NALLET** (Castres, capt) 5
- **THIERRY DUSAUTOIR** (Toulouse) 6
- **FULGENCE OUEDRAOGO** (Montpellier) 7
- **IMANOL HARINORDOQUY** (Biarritz) 8

REPLACEMENTS

Rory Best (Ulster) for Flannery (50 mins)
Gordon D'Arcy (Leinster) for P Wallace (63 mins)
Denis Leamy (Munster) for Ferris (76 mins)
Geordan Murphy (Leicester) for Kearney (80 mins)

NOT USED

Tom Court (Ulster)
Malcolm O'Kelly (Leinster)
Peter Stringer (Munster)

REPLACEMENTS

Nicolas Mas (Perpignan) for Lecouls (half-time)
Benjamin Kayser (Leicester) for Szarzewski
(59 mins)
Romain Millo-Chluski (Toulouse) for Chabal
(62 mins)
Morgan Parra (Bourgoin) for Tillous-Borde
(68 mins)
Louis Picamoles (Montpellier) for Harinordoquy
(71 mins)
Cedric Heymans (Toulouse) for Poitrenaud
(73 mins)
Benoit Baby (Clermont Auvergne) for Fritz
(78 mins)

Six Nations Championship: Round 1

	P	W	D	L	F	A	Pts
England	1	1	0	0	36	11	2
Wales	1	1	0	0	26	13	2
IRELAND	1	1	0	0	30	21	2
France	1	0	0	1	21	30	0
Scotland	1	0	0	1	13	26	0
Italy	1	0	0	1	11	36	0

ENGLAND **36** ITALY **11**

SCOTLAND **13** WALES **26**

Croke Park, February 7th, 2009. Attendance: 82,000
Referee Nigel Owen (Wales)
Touch judge Dave Pearson (England) David Changleng (Scotland)
TMO Giulio de Santis (Italy)

ITALYvIRELAND
STADIO FLAMINIO, FEBRUARY

TOMMY BOWE IS CHASED BY THE
BERGAMASCO BROTHERS

IT IS A UNITED FRONT THAT WILL MARCH IN ROME

14:02:09, STADIO FLAMINIO, LIAM TOLAND

"It was here. The battlefield was here. The Carthaginians defending the city were attacked by three Roman Legions. Carthaginians were proud and brave but they couldn't hold. They were massacred. Arab women stripped them of their tunics and their swords and lances. The soldiers lay naked in the sun, 2,000 years ago; and I was here". According to General George Smith Patton, Jr, that is. For 'Old Blood and Guts' was a staunch believer in reincarnation, where he believed he was the reincarnation of such luminaries as General Hannibal, a Roman legionnaire and a Napoleonic field marshal.

Our greatest leaders have one common characteristic which sets them apart. They all have an appreciation of the history that has brought them to this point. General Patton clearly brought this a tad too far, but for Declan Kidney entering Rome this weekend a strong understanding of the past can be his trump card.

As this is his second coming with Ireland there is a hint of Patton's reincarnation about him. Either way Ireland will win the Grand Slam in 2009 if Kidney can teach the lessons of the past.

In the aftermath of last weekend it's clear to see the imprint of Kidney's embryonic reign and the lessons learned. He has many strengths, most of which have been alluded to over recent weeks. His self-confidence that allowed world-class specialists to share his dream is clearly a huge strength. His ability to empower the players, much the way Alex Ferguson does in Manchester United is another. Of course he remains very much in charge but avoids the "spoon feeding" approach. The players will be given enough scope to arrive at "his" vision and in doing so they will be much more capable of surmounting the challenges on the pitch.

In other words they won't need an umbilical cord in times of crises. They will be able to think for themselves, confident that the coach has faith in their ability or, as Patton puts it, "if everybody is thinking alike then somebody isn't thinking". This was significant against the French, where the mental strength of the players drove them across the finish line.

I certainly believe his greatest strength is the creation of the team ethic, one for all and all for one. He has managed to achieve this by inclusion, discourse and openness where all men are created equal. In Munster he inherited a culture of Cork players and Limerick players which over time became Munster players. And in a very short time he has replicated this achievement with Ireland.

For the first time in years there is no mention of provinces. It is abundantly clear from last Saturday that the Irish team, are a team. Look at the team's reaction to the each try scorer and in particular to Brian O'Driscoll's try. They swamped him. Does he look like the forlorn leader of old? This doesn't happen by accident. Kidney clearly recognises the value in blending the provinces into one team as he did with the Cork-Limerick divide in Munster where this Irish team is now a melting pot of opportunity.

The opportunity to select Paddy Wallace at 12 was a very clever move by Kidney. He knows too well that this Italian team will attempt to neuter the Irish the only way they can. The Italians will mimic the Georgians and the Argentinians and orientate for a bruising trench war, slowing the pace of the game and attempting to dominate the corridor of power.

The Italian backs will employ a very fast defensive line that will leave Ireland with two major options. The first is to go over the onrushing defence, chip kicks (grubbers, etc) and, secondly, to go around the last defender. Considering Gordon D'Arcy's lack of real match practice it's fair to assume he's not quite at the pitch of all aspects of the inside centre role. Hence Paddy Wallace's distribution skills will afford Ireland that extra width to get Rob Kearney and co down the outside channel.

History has taught us more. When playing against lesser opposition, Ireland have in the past failed to dictate the pace. Georgia, Namibia in RWC 2007, and Italy last year, are examples of when they slowed it down. But then there was Stadio Flaminio, Rome 2007 where pace put eight tries and 51 points on a very experienced Italian side. Sunday's opposition are not as good as 2007, so we must dictate the pace at all times. That includes the times to slow down the ball, kick for the corners and outmuscle the Italians. For the major challenges ahead and in particular the English at Croke Park, the Italian match is an ideal curtain-raiser. The English are one step away from the Dean Richards style of the 1980s and 1990s. Ireland need to build on France by performing on Sunday, but to ignore the upcoming English fixture would be a wasted opportunity in Rome.

So by the final whistle in Stadio Flaminio Ireland must have dictated the pace and negated the Italian efforts to slow the ruck down allied with their ability to get outside a hard-rushing defence. Then England will be next to fall! Or as Patton puts it, "no bastard ever won a war by dying for his country; they won it by making the other dumb bastard die for his country".

Of course the greatest lesson from the past should not be wasted on Kidney, Ireland failed to secure the Six Nations Championship of 2007 because they could only beat Scotland by one point. France managed the feat by 27 points and Italy by 20 points.

And for a flavour of *Through a glass, darkly* by General George S Patton, Jr:
Still more clearly as a Roman,
Can I see the Legion close,
As our third rank moved in forward
And the short sword found our foes.
So as through a glass, and darkly
The age long strife I see
Where I fought in many guises,
Many names, but always me.

STEADY RHYTHM FROM MINOR TO MAJOR

14:02:09, STADIO FLAMINIO, **GERRY THORNLEY**

STARTING OFF, Tomás O'Leary admits he dreamed of playing in red at Croke Park. At least he scratched that itch in leading his county's minor hurlers to All-Ireland glory at Croke Park, but even then the early rugby dreams revolved around wearing red. Green and a funny shaped ball didn't enter his head.

Even as the Red Army was invented, and Munster's Magnificent Obsession took hold, making his Ireland debut against the All Blacks in Jones's Road would have seemed like the stuff of fantasy. Nevertheless, he had enough of the rugby bug in his teenage years to know the Six Nations was something special. That it came with a win, against a French side running from everywhere, made it better still. Last Tuesday he was still chuffed, using the word "great" three times in one sentence to describe last Saturday.

Now Rome. This truly is a long way from his formative years. The pity for O'Leary and Ireland, undoubtedly, is that Nick Mallett didn't have his daft-as-a-brush notion about trying to convert a 29-year-old flanker into a scrumhalf a week later. O'Leary is not remotely inclined to criticise or be sympathetic towards the plight of Mauro Bergamasco last week. Even so, like any scrumhalf, there must have been a part of O'Leary that was grateful all those hours of repetitive practice since he took up rugby at 14 hadn't been made virtually redundant.

"You never want to wish anyone else any bad, but it's a position you have to work hard on and it's a position with specific skills, passing and kicking, particularly as you go up to a higher level, and it does takes a lot of time and effort. But I suppose you get more satisfaction when you improve then. When I first started playing I was 14 or 15. The oval ball was kinda different from what I was used to but you just have to have time and perseverance to get used to the skills."

Needless to say, as even the dogs in Piazza Navona are probably aware by now, he's the son of Seánie, winner of four senior All Ireland hurling medals and a three time All Star, the first three of those titles at the ground his son adorned last week and the last in Thurles in 1984 - the GAA's centenary year. His father retired then, a year after Tomás was born. "I've seen bits and pieces on video and stuff." His father doesn't like to hog any of his son's limelight, and while Seánie doesn't pretend to be an expert on rugby, he has passed on useful advice on how to deal with high-pressure games. "He never really coached me, so he never really got too animated on the sidelines with me. I probably wouldn't have listened to him if he did," quips O'Leary, "but he's always been a calming influence. The same with my mother. They've been good influences on my career."

Having been to St Patrick's Boys School in Gardner's Hill where, like most primary schools, rugby was non existent and hurling, football and soccer were the sports, O'Leary was sent to CBC Cork, largely for geographical reasons. Initially, with his natural speed, O'Leary played a few games on the wing before being moved closer to the action by "one of the teachers". He can't remember who was responsible, perhaps out of diplomacy. "There's a couple of them fighting over it now. Either Russell Foley or Tony Wall, they're both claiming it, so I'll leave it between them to fight that one out," he says with a smile.

He continued to play hurling and football with Erin's Own until he was 19, playing with the Cork minor hurling team for two years and captaining them to an All Ireland title in 2001 at the age of 17. He then played a year with the county's under-21s. Meantime, he and rugby quickly took a hold of each other. In his second season, the Christians' juniors beat Rockwell in the Munster final at Thomond Park. In his senior cup year he had less joy, being obliged to play at outhalf in a semi-final defeat to bitter rivals Pres. "Murray Kidd and Peter Melia were coaching us and they got a notion I could play outhalf. Duncan Williams, who is in Munster at the moment, was in fourth year and we had no real outhalf, so they threw me in there. The goalkicking wasn't great and we lost, partly due to my goalkicking," he recalls with a wry but broadening smile. "Well, mainly due to my goalkicking."

His father didn't put the slightest pressure on him to focus more on his hurling or football. "There was certainly a bit of pressure from some hurling people, just the diehards really, but my mam and dad encouraged me to go for it. I talked with them, and I wanted to play for Munster and play professional rugby, and they were delighted I had that ambition. I knew myself, and they knew, that worst-case scenario, you'd give it three or four years and you're still only 22-23. You can always go back hurling. "My grandmother, my dad's mum, probably would have been the most disappointed, but she's a massive rugby fan now. I'd say she never watched a game of rugby in her life until a couple of years ago but at least she saw me play minor for Cork."

The year before that All Ireland minor success, he'd been on a losing team in the final against Galway, so there was the additional revenge in denying Galway a three in a row. "We had a brilliant team. We had John Gardiner, who has gone on to play for Cork, and Shane Murphy, Cian O'Connor and the two Ciarán Murphys, and Setanta Ó hAilpín was on that team as well. So we had a very good outfit. It wasn't a brilliant game but we won by three or four points, just got the win basically, but it was a brilliant win."

And the, eh, current mess/impasse/ imbroglio in Cork hurling? Needless to say, he has to toe a fairly diplomatic line amid such a political minefield, though understandably you sense his sympathy is with the players, some of whom are former Rebel teammates from his minor days. "There's a fair few Cork lads (in the Irish squad) and we get a lot of slagging from the rest of them. It's a right mess. Everybody wants to see Cork with the best team on the pitch and challenging for an All Ireland. I don't think Cork or Tipperary will challenge Kilkenny without a full side. Obviously Gerald (McCarthy) might be doing his best and he wants all the players there as well to challenge, but it doesn't look like both parties can work together any more."

O'Leary's early sporting days would be fairly commonplace and he says his Gaelic playing days were "a great place to develop your skills; speed, hand-eye co-ordination." Even so, the balancing act was proving difficult. Not alone had he his Erin's Own hurling and football sides and his Christians rugby sides, but there were county underage teams and the Munster and the Irish Schools sides to further complicate things. Understanding from coaches in all codes was required. "When you're young you don't really think about burnout, you're full of energy. Overall, it was great, and I definitely wouldn't change it."

But it was almost a relief having a gun pointing to his head, albeit in the form of an offer of a year with the IRFU Academy. He was 19. It was decision time. Quite candidly, he admits: "The fact there was an opportunity to play professional rugby if you were lucky enough was the defining factor. I love rugby and I loved it at that stage as well, but I loved hurling and football just as much. The over-riding factor was that I could be a professional athlete."

Munster were taking off too, though an early landmark came at the Under-21 World Cup in Scotland in 2004, when an Irish team featuring himself, Jamie Heaslip, Tommy Bowe and Denis Fogarty, beat France and Australia en route to the final before losing to New Zealand. "That opened my eyes that we weren't a million miles away from the top nations and from gaining professional contracts."

He takes pleasure in seeing his teammates from that tournament breaking through as well. As to why it took him so long? He smiles and sums it up in two words. Peter Stringer. "Strings has been a great player and is still playing great stuff. You're not going to get rid of a player like Peter Stringer. He's a legend of Munster and Irish rugby, the most capped scrumhalf in Irish history. So I had to be patient but I think my game has come on more because I had to work harder behind Peter, and to

LUKE FITZGERALD CROSSES FOR HIS SECOND TRY OF THE GAME AT STADIO FLAMINIO

have him at training, you're learning bits from him too. So I think it's been beneficial for me."

Described as a relatively quiet if good humoured presence in the Munster dressingroom, O'Leary is a dedicated and driven son of Munster. Last season, his third with them, was his breakthrough year, although the season before, 2006-07, he was virtually an ever-present in the Magners League. Of his three Heineken Cup starts before last season, one had been on the wing, one at centre and one at scrumhalf; a slightly harrowing baptism in the defeat away to Sale at the outset of the 2005-06 campaign.

But it was away to Gloucester in last season's quarter-finals that O'Leary's career took off, as he readily concedes. "The game against Ulster, before that game, was a big game for me, and Declan and Tony McGahan just said, 'Keep doing what you're doing', and luckily things went well for me then." He credits the improvement in his passing to Garryowen's Scottish director of rugby Greg Oliver, and his Dolphin coach, David O'Mahony. "I had played with Con for a year on the wing and I was getting a bit pissed off, because I wanted to play scrumhalf, so I moved to Dolphin and Dave O'Mahony there was brilliant for me.

"And then in the last year or two Greg has continued on that work - he works with all the scrumhalves in Munster. It's something I need to keep working on and improve, the same as all aspects of my game, defence, kicking, everything; not to get too hung up on it but I need to keep working on it."

Whereas he'd been on the bench in the '06 Heineken Cup final, last season he was a pivotal part in the triumph. "To play in it, in the Millennium Stadium and packed with Munster fans, was unbelievable, and against Toulouse as well. A brilliant day, and brilliant memories going back home with the trophy. It gives you a hunger to have more success and it gives you a hunger to play at a higher level. "And that's what I want to do, I want to get to as high a level as I can and play for Ireland and play against the best sides in the world, and see how good I am and see how I can handle myself." Son of Seánie is handling himself just fine so far.

NOT PRETTY BUT ITALIAN JOB IS DONE

16:02:09, STADIO FLAMINIO, **GERRY THORNLEY**

ITALIAN JOB done, as Ireland duly came, saw and conquered Italy in what has become their eternal fashion hereabouts. Maintaining their five-try average in a typically sunkissed Stadio Flaminio from their previous four visits here, Ireland thus went to the top of a formative Six Nations table ahead of Wales on points' difference. It's becoming a little harder not to get a little giddy. As with previous treks, though, the scoreline assuredly gives little indication of the travail and pain Ireland had to endure before getting there in the end. In truth, but not entirely surprisingly, Ireland did not play especially well but, in the heel of the hunt, they thought their way through this one as much as fought their way through it.

Needless to say, with England in town on Saturday week, no better man that Declan Kidney to keep our giddiness in check. Though still somewhat limited, England's defence showed improvement in making Wales sweat for their 23-15, despite taking their costly tally of yellow cards to eight in four games. "I thought that they improved 300 per cent from the previous week. They've really come on," ventured Kidney, before making a telling contrast with the ramshackle, overplayed English team that came to Croke Park in round three two years ago. "It's important with the new agreement that they have a week off and it gives Martin a chance they didn't have heretofore to improve for two weeks time. They'll have learned from today. Ireland-England games you look forward to in a kind of masochistic way. You know how god they are. The size of the challenge has improved enormously and they'll be eyeing us as a target."

Ireland had sought to play more of a ball-in-hand, offloading game - kicking the ball only eight per cent of the time. But in trying to force things, it was getting them nowhere in the face of some fierce defending and they were indebted to an intercept try by Tommy Bowe to turn a 6-0 deficit into a one point lead. Gradually, they narrowed their focus, played more territory and wore Italy out, only varnishing the scoreline late on. "We did well to adapt in the 20 minutes before half-time," enthused Kidney. "Now whether that adaptation was forced upon us by the injury and yellow card? But that's when I thought we were at our best, when we just said, 'right let's do something different here'. That's what I liked."

A stiff arm, neck high hit on Rob Kearney by Andrea Masi inside the first 30 seconds, welcomed the Irish fullback into the game and set the tone for a slightly frenzied and madcap opening half. The Italian fullback became the first of three players to be yellow carded as Ronan O'Gara (who had a decidedly mixed bag in the first 40 but regrouped thereafter) and Salvatore Perugini followed him to the bin. That said, O'Gara's tug of Masi's jersey after having his own kick charged down was one of the better yellow cards ever conceded - for it may have prevented Italy extending their lead from 9-7 to 16-7.

In the event, it also proved a blessing in disguise for, coupled with the unfortunate Paddy Wallace departing with another facial injury, it left Ireland with no choice but to keep knocking penalties into the corner in the build-up to Luke Fitzgerald's try bang on half-time. Championship moments, as Matt Williams calls them, and followed soon after by David Wallace muscling over in trademark style through some beaten blue jerseys, the game was up.

Although the glory and the tries went mostly to the backs - Fitzgerald scoring two, with Tommy Bowe and Brian O'Driscoll adding one each - the pack will arguably derive more satisfaction from gradually subduing the Italian forwards. Ireland cut down on their ratio of kicking and, with large tracts of territorial dominance, kept the ball in hand much more, but their moves and attempts to introduce more of an offloading game struggled in the face of Italy's rush defence.

Nearing half-time, in the pivotal period of the game, Ireland adopted a different strategy, pounding away at the Italians' defence closer in through 19 phases. Eventually Stephen Ferris made the play for Fitzgerald to score with a razor sharp trailer. Ferris was magnificent, positively revelling in the arm wrestle Italy sought to engage Ireland in. He was the one gaining the yards when they were the hardest to accrue, running some superb lines and pumping his legs in contact.

Paul O'Connell was, well, Paul O'Connell in true lead-from-the-front style and for almost half an hour it was as if the Irish forwards simply kept

TROUBLE ON THE DOUBLE FOR PADDY WALLACE

ownership of the ball. So it was that Wallace grew more into the game, and even for his try in the 46th minute, the Italians looked out on their feet. So it was no great surprise when Fitzgerald and O'Driscoll waltzed in for tries against opponents who had long since wilted. Peter Stringer, too, could feel happy with his contribution, Ireland scoring three of their five tries when he was on the pitch.

Surprisingly, given the innumerable bruises and bangs which the Irish players incurred, Kidney appeared none too concerned about the various injuries to Stephen Ferris (a blood injury), Marcus Horan (a bang on the back of the head), Rob Kearney (calf tightened up) and poor old Paddy Wallace - a wound around one eye which required 16 stitches against France has now been replicated on the other eye.

No doubt the Irish coach was also mightily grateful for an additional week's rest, and may look to have Gordon D'Arcy play for Leinster next week as well, perhaps, as some of the other subs. But not too many more. "We'll decide whether we need to freshen things up for the next match or whether we should play a few in the Magners League. It's brilliant to be involved but there's nothing won already. Experience has told me that in the Heineken Cup, you could have two wins but that's all it is. A huge game for us next. Every game is like a cup final." It is now.

IRELAND'S PATIENCE AND PERSEVERANCE PAY

16:02:09, STADIO FLAMINIO, **GERRY THORNLEY**

ITALY 9 IRELAND 38

IN THE end, it followed a fairly dog-eared script. The Azzurri, as ever, gave the men in green a fair old bruising before their efforts subsided and Ireland showed their class to pull away far more comfortably than had looked likely in a wildly ill-disciplined first half.

At that point there had been three men in the bin and the penalty count was 12-7 to Ireland, ultimately finishing 18-12. Yet it wasn't particularly dirty, just that such was the Italians' fire and fury that they conceded penalties with impunity, particularly at the breakdown. Ireland struggled to establish any sort of rhythm or control as Italy's rush defence forced spillages and turnovers from attempted offloads. Ireland regrouped before the break though, with both sides down to 14 men, and painstakingly went through three minutes and 19 phases of ball retention to regain the lead for the second time in the match. They never had to do so again.

Stephen Ferris, whose barnstorming physicality had proved more than a match for the hosts, was the instigator in chief of that try. Credit for subduing Italy goes firstly to the pack, where Paul O'Connell took on a mountain of work, and with the strong running of Rob Kearney, roving intelligence of Tommy Bowe and dynamic pace of Luke Fitzgerald coming more into play: there were also some exquisite moments from Brian O'Driscoll.

Chris White soon established his rule over the game. After Tommy Bowe's strong chase and hit on Sergio Parisse, from Tomás O'Leary's excellent box kick, encouraged the Irish backs to give the ball some air and width, Rob Kearney was nearly beheaded by Andrea Masi. However, in the next two minutes Ireland conceded as many full penalties (two) as they had in 80 minutes the previous week. Jerry Flannery and Donncha O'Callaghan were rightly penalised for not staying on their feet when John Hayes picked and went but, more to the point, given the extra man, opting for pick and go looked a curious choice of tactic.

Penalties at 40 to 45 metres into the breeze were beyond Ronan O'Gara's range and he missed a penalty to touch before another, easily won by David Wallace at the tail, was picked off by Sergio Parisse. With David Wallace pinged for not rolling away and O'Callaghan playing the ball from an offside position, the Azzurri were given the further encouragement of two Luke McLean penalties either side of Masi returning. Ireland, unsure of themselves, needed something out of the blue and Bowe provided it. Picking off a flicked pass by Mirco Bergamasco, he broke Griffen's tackle and stayed just out of reach of all chasers in a 60 metre dash to the line. O'Gara tapped over the conversion.

McLean nudged Italy back in front after a high tackle by O'Callaghan on Fabio Ongaro and, though Italy were now being penalised at virtually every breakdown, O'Gara was rightly binned for tugging back Gonzalo Canale after the centre blocked down his kick. Relief came by way of McLean missing his easiest of four kicks and a searing break out by O'Leary. Paddy Wallace had to make way for a blood injury which may have turned out to be a blessing. With Peter Stringer in at scrumhalf, O'Leary playing at outhalf and no goalkicker, twice O'Driscoll opted to go to the corner. It yielded an immediate reward when repeat barging through at lineouts led to Salvatore Perugini being binned.

Back Ireland came to the corner for another sequence of rumbles off O'Connell's take. For many of the intervening 19 phases Ireland went backwards in the face of fierce Italian defending; O'Driscoll juggling with a hospital pass to keep the move alive. Stringer remained calm at the base however and it was the magnificent Ferris who came up with the definitive play, steaming onto the ball and calling for Stringer's delayed pop to break Paul Griffen's tackle and free his hands for an offload to Luke Fitzgerald, who ran an alert support trailer. Kearney knocked over the routine conversion from in front of the posts for the final play of the half.

It was a massive swing in the match, worthy of more than a mere seven points. It also underlined the virtues of patience and control. O'Gara twice kicked with accuracy to the corner and though the Italian lineout held firm, O'Driscoll danced in midfield and freed his hands for Jamie Heaslip to make a huge rumble to within a couple of metres of the line before he was brilliantly hauled down by Matteo Pratichetti. It merely delayed the inevitable though.

With Gonzalo Canale down injured, O'Callaghan, Bowe and Heaslip all set up ruck ball before David Wallace broke the tackles of Carlo Festuccia, Tommaso Reato and Pratichetti to score. O'Gara converted. Italy were beginning to unravel now amid a surfeit of replacements and Ireland cut loose for a late double whammy. First Luke Fitzgerald exchanged a quick throw with Gordon D'Arcy to sprint over from 40 metres out and then O'Driscoll picked off an ambitious skip pass by Masi to run in another intercept try, O'Gara converting both.

STILL VERY MUCH ON TRACK, NOW BRING ON ENGLAND

16:02:09, STADIO FLAMINIO, **LIAM TOLAND**

I'LL GIVE the first words to General George S Patton Jr. "A man must know his destiny . . . if he does not recognise it, then he is lost. By this I mean, once, twice, or at the very most, three times, fate will reach out and tap a man on the shoulder. If he has the imagination, he will turn around and fate will point out to him what fork in the road he should take, if he has the guts, he will take it."

Fate is now tapping on Declan Kidney's shoulder following this difficult but winning performance in Rome where a brave but limited Italian side deserved more. However, individual class kept Ireland nicely on track. Further encouragement can be gleaned from the countless occasions we bravely fought against sides in the past but drifted away in the end. So it was very satisfying to score five tries against very stiff opposition. Bonus point anyone?

Kidney's counterpart, Nick Mallett is a coach not afraid to experiment, but he returned to the Italian/Argentinian tactics of old which afforded the Italians a chance to beat someone other than Scotland this season. At no stage was the challenge in Rome understated. We knew in advance that the breakdown would have a major effect on Rob Kearney and company.

With a front five as grizzled as the Italians they were always going to disrupt the outside backs. Lesson learned? I hope so because reflecting on the challenges that lie ahead, Ireland must produce a predictable flow of possession. The Italians were so ferocious at the breakdown that the Irish backrow, in particular Jamie Heaslip, was forced to ignore the more pleasant task of open field running in order to secure possession. But in successfully ensuring the flow of ball to Tomás O'Leary, the Irish backrow displayed the dexterity of thought that augers well for the weeks ahead. Regarding the management of the breakdown, Peter Stringer's cameo role before half-time provided food for thought. He continues to be much faster at the base.

The Italian pack was well served by the sensible decision to play Paul Griffen, a scrumhalf, at scrumhalf. He teamed up nicely with Australian-born Luke McLean. The high energy of Mauro Bergamasco and especially number eight Sergio Parisse transformed their performance from last week. So much so that by the 34th minute, although Italy were two to one ahead on the sin binnings, 11 to seven ahead on penalties conceded and were way behind in possession, managing only 33 per cent, they were still ahead on the scoreboard at 9-7.

Worrying? Absolutely! Ireland displayed tactical naivety in failing to get outside an extremely committed Italian four-up defence. Instead they resigned themselves to run at fatties. That's a pity as Kearney's first three touches resulted in three very strong attacking runs. It appeared at that stage that Ireland were in the mood to start like Wales did against the English on Saturday. But it wasn't to be. Not to worry because there are 80 minutes in every match and Ireland built towards a victory through an excellent lineout and a solid scrum that produced a huge dividend in penalties.

Marcus Horan can be very pleased with his performance, earning several penalties against Martin Castrogiovanni. However, fewer rucks might have made the journey easier. There was no shortage of brave ball carriers, but too often they ended up on the deck. Contrast that to Saturday and the Welsh who may hit the deck but they rarely allow the ball to do the same as it's offloaded long before the opposition can get their hands on it. If the breakdown was the biggest challenge for the Irish backline, attack was the next, particularly in the first half.

To my mind Paddy Wallace was not utilised to his strengths and as time wore on Gordon D'Arcy's entry was inevitable. Maybe it's a Kidney tactic but why aren't the Irish back three brought into play more often? Look what happened when Luke Fitzgerald popped up in the 39th minute off a ruck to complete the excellent work by Stephen Ferris and Stringer. When Ireland did go wide at times it was lateral, allowing the Italians to force the attack towards the touch-line. We need more consistent decoys, fixing the defence.

I suppose based on this weekend the key question remains: can Wales be beaten? Their entry into the Millennium Stadium was slow, measured

BRIAN O'DRISCOLL CAN'T FIND ANY PURSUERS

and full of self confidence, but a struggling English caused them problems. This Irish side has so many gears in it that perfecting the breakdown and backline angle of attack will reap huge rewards. It was a very challenging afternoon which the Irish met, so bring on England!

As an aside, what about the men in the middle? Chris White of England had a very different take on the breakdown to his assistant and last week's referee Nigel Owens. And certainly South African referee Jonathan Kaplan had a monumentally different view on Saturday in the middle of the Welsh-English fixture. Altogether very confusing!

MAGICAL MEMORY FOR FITZGERALD

16:02:09, STADIO FLAMINIO, PADDY AGNEW

LUKE FITZGERALD had not visited Rome since he was a young lad, but after his two tries in Ireland's emphatic 38-9 win over Italy yesterday he freely admits to looking forward to his next trip to the Eternal City. He might have been here this weekend on a serious "mission", but he still took time to walk around the Centro Storico on Saturday night. Given the way he played yesterday, the sights of ancient Rome have clearly done his rugby game no harm.

Looking sharp and fresh, not at all like someone who had just played through a tough physical game, he offered an understandably upbeat post-match analysis. He was not saying it, but the sensation is that this Irish team is beginning to build up some serious momentum. "I think, overall, it was a good old trip to Rome. They are a very physically imposing team and difficult to break down. You saw that last week against England even if the scoreline did not show it - a lot of England's points came from Italian mistakes.

"Physical games like this one are some of the most enjoyable ones, especially when you come out on the right side. But you have to work really hard at it, you have to outwork them and I think that's what we did today, there was massive work done by the pack. They put their heart and soul into it and, thank God, we came out on the right side."

Fitzgerald felt Ireland were not flattered by the final scoreline. "I thought we took our opportunities very well and I would hate to seem disrespectful of the Italians by saying that they were no good. I thought they played very well, but we took our opportunities really well and that was more a testament to us than to them." He agreed that his first try just before half-time was probably the killer blow as far as Italy were concerned.

The impact of a try that took the score from 9-7 in Italy's favour to 9-14 was doubly crippling, not only because it came just before half-time but also because it came after five minutes of sustained Irish pressure that the plucky Italian defence simply could not stand up to. "I think that try was a killer blow because we had held onto the ball for so long and that was very draining for them. If we hadn't got a score then and they had gone into half-time still in the lead, that would have given them a massive boost. But it went the other way and we got a massive boost just before half-time."

Fitzgerald's thoughts now turn to the next assignment, against England. "England are always tough to beat no matter how they are playing at the moment. I know they are getting a bit of stick from their own media, but from what I can see, they look very imposing, very physically tough. And they have mixed those qualities with some fantastic finishers like Paul Sackey and Mark Cueto, so I think they have a good blend and they will be tough to beat.

"I thought England were a bit unlucky against Wales yesterday, even if the Welsh were clearly very good and took their chances well . . . if one or two things had gone England's way it could have been a very different day.

JOB WELL DONE SO FAR ON ROAD TO IMMORTALITY

17:02:09, GERRY THORNLEY

TEMPTING FATE is always a risky business as far as Irish rugby is concerned. After all, it's been 61 years since Ireland slam-dunked all and sundry for the one and only time and it's been 24 years since their last of a relatively meagre 10 outright titles. Only France, in their 40-year wait for a first title, have had a longer barren period to endure. So, two down, three to go. Not even halfway there yet. Halfway to a possible tilt at immortality.

If nothing else, though, Declan Kidney and his Irish Brains Trust have restored confidence to the Irish rugby team and restored the smiles on the faces of the players and those supporting them. Coming from where they were for much of the previous 19 months, that alone is an astounding achievement.

There will have been a mite too many errors for comfort in the opening half-hour or so in Rome when they come to view the video, but overall the management and players alike can feel content with a job well done so far.

Kidney appears to be pulling the strings masterfully and not alone has he decided superbly on his back-up staff, but he has delegated as well. A massive dollop of credit so far must go to forwards' coach Gert Smal, for the set-pieces have been the bedrock of the two wins to date.

Clearly Kidney landed a plum coach in the former Springboks number eight and World Cup-winning forwards' coach. A relatively quiet individual with a dry wit, Smal commands respect when he does speak and the players talk of him as combining an old-style motivational approach with technical expertise. The solidity of the scrum is as much, apparently, the confidence he has imbued in the players as anything.

Defensive coach Les Kiss will have harder games to plan for than against a relatively impotent Italy, but not only did the defence keep their try-line intact, the quicker line speed under the new regime also contributed to two interceptions and 14 points.

And, miracle of miracles, Ireland are scoring tries again. The rejuvenated Brian O'Driscoll and the outside three are becoming increasingly more influential. Their conversion rate of chances into tries has been quite clinical, and in stark contrast to Leinster's failure to take their chances in January.

Leinster backs' coach Alan Gaffney has taken none too kindly to the relatively slight questioning of the Leinster and Irish backplay, and primarily their depth. But Ireland certainly seemed to be playing with more width and depth again on Saturday, especially in the second half when adapting to Italy's rush defence. Indeed, at times, they almost seemed to be a little too deep.

Along with Wales, Ireland look the most potent side in the tournament again, although that partly depends on which French side turns up on any given day. Or perhaps that should be where they turn up, for it is becoming increasingly apparent that Stade de France gives them a form of stage fright. The boos which greeted them at half-time on Saturday against the Scots (half-time for heaven's sake!) brought to mind Bernard Laporte's description of the Stade crowd as bourgeoise shits.

If there is no slam winner, and both history and the bookies' odds make this the likeliest outcome still, at least Ireland's healthy winning margin in Rome leaves their points differential in a healthy state were the destination of the title to come down to that.

Another way of dampening hopes is to take a closer look at Italy - and the suspicion lurks that the Azzurri are the weakest link in the Six Nations. Italy desperately need to have two regionalised, largely indigenous sides competing in the Magners League, and for the betterment of the European and global game the Celtic nations and the IRB have a duty to make this happen, as now looks likely.

The improvements wrought by both England and Scotland in round two suggest this is still far from a clearly demarcated tournament destined for a winner-takes-all shoot-out in Cardiff.

One way in which Kidney has much in common with Eddie O'Sullivan is how they talk up the opposition, but this is fairly standard head-coach speak, for not only does it make expectations more realistic, it's also part of treating the opposition with respect.

The dust had scarcely settled in the Stadio Flaminio and Kidney was reminding us in contrast to two years ago England's players would be rested from club duty next weekend as a result of the accord between the clubs and the RFU. The contrast with two years ago is indeed stark. Then, as now,

England came to Croke Park in round three, but whereas Ireland's players were rested from Magners League duty the weekend before following their win away to Wales and home defeat to France, the Premiership went ahead with a full programme the preceding Sunday.

Poor Brian Ashton. Having presided over Ireland's record defeat to England, he duly coached the injury-ravaged Red Rose to their heaviest defeat against Ireland that day in completing a unique Test double. Afterwards, Ashton pointed out that due to the recovery from the previous Sunday's exertions, a travel day and a six-day turnaround, effectively they only had one full session that week. And, recalling how Shaun Perry's notional pass to Jonny Wilkinson was picked off by Isaac Boss late on, they certainly played like strangers.

They weren't by any means a team of lightweights, but only three of that starting XV - Wilkinson, Phil Vickery and Martin Corry - lined up in the World Cup final nine months later. This, though, will be different. England will be vastly better prepared under Martin Johnson and against Wales had improved immeasurably defensively with the inclusion of Joe Worsley, amid signs also that Riki Flutey and Delon Armitage are adding something going forward.

Furthermore, and perhaps just as significantly, while there is always something special about England coming to town and all the more so with a Saturday tea-time crowd that rediscovered its voice and belief in Team Ireland just over a week ago, the hype and rich sense of history attached to England's first visit to Croke Park simply cannot be replicated. That was a complete one-off in so many ways, and the Irish players were also looking to atone for that defeat to France.

The prize this time is a purely rugby one.

ITALY

9-38

IRELAND

McLean pen	5:05	
McLean pen	16:31	
	20:06	Bowe try
	21:23	O'Gara con
McLean pen	27:00	
	45:50	Fitzgerald try
	46:52	Kearney con
	H-T	
	6:4	D Wallace try
	8:0	O'Gara con
	12:11	O'Gara pen
	45:39	Fitzgerald try
	47:18	O'Gara con
	48:18	O'Driscoll try
	49:08	O'Gara con

15 ANDREA MASI (Biarritz)
14 KAINE ROBERTSON (Viadana)
13 GONZALO CANALE (Clermont)
12 MIRCO BERGAMASCO (Stade Francais)
11 MATTEO PRATICHETTI (Calvisano)
10 LUKE McLEAN (Calvisano)
9 PAULGRIFFEN (Colomiers)
1 SALVATORE PERUGINI (Toulouse)
2 FABIO ONGARO (Saracens)
3 MARTIN CASTROGIOVANNI (Leicester)
4 SANTIAGO DELLAPE (Toulon)
5 TOMMASO REATI (Rovigo)
6 ALESSANDRO ZANNI (Calvisano)
7 MAURO BERGAMASCO (Stade Francais)
8 SERGIO PARISSE (Stade Francais, capt)

ROB KEARNEY (Leinster) **15**
TOMMY BOWE (Ospreys) **14**
BRIAN O'DRISCOLL (Leinster, capt) **13**
PADDY WALLACE (Ulster) **12**
LUKE FITZGERALD (Leinster) **11**
RONAN O'GARA (Munster) **10**
TOMÁS O'LEARY (Munster) **9**
MARCUS HORAN (Munster) **1**
JERRY FLANNERY (Munster) **2**
JOHN HAYES (Munster) **3**
DONNCHA O'CALLAGHAN (Munster) **4**
PAUL O'CONNELL (Munster) **5**
STEPHEN FERRIS (Ulster) **6**
DAVID WALLACE (Munster) **7**
JAMIE HEASLIP (Leinster) **8**

REPLACEMENTS

A Bacchetti (Rovigo) for Robertson (19 mins)
Carlos Nieto (Gloucester) for Castrogiovanni (33 mins)
Carlo Festuccia (Racing, Paris) for Ongaro (42 mins)
Gonzalo Garcia (Calvisano) for Canale (48 mins)
Carlo Del Fava (Ulster) for Dellape (48 mins)
Josh Sole (Viadana) for Reati (48 mins)
G Tonialatti (Capitalina) for McLean (72)

REPLACEMENTS

Gordon D'Arcy (Leinster) for P Wallace (42 mins)
Tom Court (Ulster) for Horan (58 mins)
Rory Best (Ulster) for Flannery (65 mins)
Denis Leamy (Munster) for Ferris (70 mins)
Peter Stringer (Munster) for O'Leary (80 mins)
Geordan Murphy (Leicester) for Kearney (85 mins)
Malcolm O'Kelly (Leinster) for O'Connell (86 mins)

Six Nations Championship: Round 2

	P	W	D	L	F	A	Pts
IRELAND	2	2	0	0	68	30	4
Wales	2	2	0	0	49	28	4
England	2	1	0	1	51	34	2
France	2	1	0	1	43	43	2
Scotland	2	0	0	2	26	48	0
Italy	2	0	0	2	20	74	0

FRANCE **22** SCOTLAND **13**
WALES **23** ENGLAND **15**

Stadio Flaminio, February 15th, 2009. Attendance: 32,000
Referee Chris White (England)
Touch judge Nigel Owens (Wales) Romain Poite (France)
TMO Graham Hughes (England)

IRELANDVENGLAND

CROKE PARK, FEBRUARY

DENIS LEAMY MANHANDLES ENGLAND'S TOM CROFT

THIS TIME ENGLAND FREE TO PLAY DIFFERENT ROLE

28:02:09, CROKE PARK, **KEITH DUGGAN**

England again! Much has changed since that chill and hazy February evening two years ago when 15 men in pristine white shirts emerged from the tunnel of the Hogan Stand in Croke Park, beaten before they ever took the field. In retrospect, the men wearing the red rose of England that night hadn't a chance. As John Pullin immortally remarked of his own English team that showed up in Dublin during the tense months of 1972: "We mightn't always win, but at least we turn up."

Two years ago, an English rugby team turned up for what was, as they say, a night to remember. But remembered for what? It is time to acknowledge that Ireland versus England, Six Nations 2007, was one of the weirdest evenings in the history of Irish sport. How could the English have won on an evening aquiver with the weight of a dark episode in Irish history being righted - through a rugby match?

Gamely, the boys from the Home Counties appeared on the field. Englishmen, back on Croke Park, so many decades after . . . lest we forget . . . uncertain of how they would be received. The sight of them standing there brought to mind Captain George's description in Blackadder Goes Forth of his pals as they signed up in August 1914: "Crashingly superb bunch of blokes. Fine, clean-limbed; even our acne had a strange nobility about it."

They walked out onto the field fully accepting their meek roles in what, with the distance of a full two years, seems an even more bizarre pageant of mixed-up history, sentimentalism, boozy national pride, slick marketing, incessant anthem singing and the vaguely uncomfortable sense that a rugby match had become a mass rally for Irish jingoism. Gravely, the English boys stood shoulder to shoulder as God Save the Queen resounded around the stadium. They understood the significance of the moment. They understood their presence in Croke Park was a big deal, that the idea of St George's flag fluttering over the red-bricked terraces of Dublin city evoked keen emotions in the Irish.

And they understood that in the dim and distant past, when Europe was recovering from one world war and assembling the various attitudes and philosophies that would set it on an irrevocable path towards a second, that Englishmen in uniform had once done something terrible in this ground. They knew because they were given a history lecture on Bloody Sunday in the days before the game. Nobody can be certain how that little talk ended, but it might have been along the lines of: "All in all chaps, it might be best if you finished second best in the match."

So a few lonely-sounding English voices loyally sang their tribute to queen and country and the glories of lost empire in this old sporting theatre, the last bastion of Irish nationalism. And then the miracle: you could hear a penny drop. That is what we said afterwards, pouring out of the ground and into the super-pubs. The Irish stood up and stood silent and allowed the guests of the nation to sing it out. And we were proud of ourselves.

A bit teary, in fact. We are nothing if not a sentimental lot and never pass up a chance to celebrate ourselves. Look at us now, we marvelled: a mature, sophisticated, modern country. And rich! When it came to our turn for the anthems - Amhrán na bhFiann for Southerners, Phil Coulter's best for Our Friends in the North - we gave it socks. Shook the foundations of "Croker". In fact, we proclaimed, the old girl never had such a good time in all her years. The GAA opened up their hall but it took the rugby crowd to show them how to hold a real dance.

On to the game, and there was only one team in it. Ireland thundered into England and it soon became clear Albion's challenge was pale. As the match turned into a rout, the atmosphere was raucous and jubilant and it thirsted for more scores, it thirsted for the sight and sensation of an England team crushed in this old theatre of new dreams.

The English team played their part, the English newspapers said all the rights things - were glowing in their praise of us, in fact - and, as their aeroplanes wheeled high over Dublin Bay to deliver them back to Blighty, they must have scratched their heads and wondered what the hell it was all about. If ever the English were destined not to understand the Irish, it was that weekend.

But the whole occasion was all just plain wrong. It was manufactured emotion. The big problem with everything that happened that night was that it overlooked the huge, glaring fact that what happened on Bloody Sunday belongs to GAA culture. It is part of their history. True, there were GAA men in the crowd delighted their stadium could play host to this international sports fixture. But equally, there was a significant minority of GAA people who rued - and continue to - the day when Croke Park was opened up.

And there was still another element who could never quite understand how the memory of what was a real and terrible atrocity could be married to what was a finely tuned international sports event, as if it were somehow part of the programme of events along with the three course dinners, the advertising and the television hoopla.It is easy to understand why the night mattered so much to the Irish rugby players. The hype and moral expectation in the days before the game was all but unbearable: whatever about the public forgiving them had they lost, it is unlikely that they would have forgiven themselves. The players were as this group have been throughout: committed and blazing with pride, proud to play for Ireland.

The fault was with the rest of us. It was with everyone who contributed to the myth that Ireland versus England 2007 marked some sort of natural understanding between two nations with a close and bloody past. It was never that. Ireland got carried away with the conjured portents that the evening held and the English sportingly played along. Then, they had no choice to do otherwise.

Two years on and England come back, the underdogs again and thorns in those roses they wear on their breasts. Martin Johnson could recite Henry V's St Crispin's Day's speech for all anyone cares this evening: there is not so much talk about Croke Park as the hallowed ground this time around. That must be a relief for the English lads. At least they won't have to listen solemnly to Irish history lessons. At least they won't have to run into a stadium full of 70,000 Paddies in High Pomposity mode. And at least they won't have to feel guilty about being English.

WELL-GROUNDED ATHLETES FEELING AT HOME IN CROKE PARK

28:02:09, CROKE PARK, **GERRY THORNLEY**

Most likely there's never been such a Gaelic Games infused Irish rugby team to take the field in a Six Nations game as there is today, and that seems particularly appropriate as Ireland face up to a second and last encounter with England at Croke Park amid this brief window in Irish sporting history. Nothing embodied Ireland's unforgettable 43-13 win over England two years ago than Shane Horgan fielding Ronan O'Gara's crossfield kick in applying the coup de grace.

Indeed, the Croker effect must only add to the pain which the likes of Horgan and Girvan Dempsey are feeling at missing out so far this season. Like Dempsey, today's replacement fullback Geordan Murphy is another whose brilliance under the high ball was at least in part honed on GAA fields in his formative Newbridge years, and in this regard perhaps nobody betrays his GAA roots more ably than Rob Kearney.

"I was lucky in a way that the two seasons differed, so as soon as the rugby season was over I was in to the thick of the Gaelic season," he reflects, having started playing Gaelic football at seven or eight with Grange National School, progressing to Cooley Kickhams at under-14s. In his last of three years on the Louth minors they were beaten by Dublin at the Leinster semi-final stage in a replay, having come within a kick of reaching the final.

"If we hadn't been beaten by Dublin I would have played at Croke Park which would have been unbelievable, wouldn't it?" he says, still nursing the sense of regret. "But it wasn't to be. We were beating them in the first game and they equalised in the last minute of the game. Not even a minute to go. It was the last kick of the game. Then in the replay they beat us by two points, and we had a good side too. It was a killer. That was the time before Leinster academies, and while I wouldn't say Gaelic was my first love, it was a big, big sport for me at the time."

Indeed, his last match for Cooley Kickhams was in the Louth county final, a game for which he delayed signing his Leinster Academy contract. "We were beaten by the local team from St Pat's, and there was big rivalry between those two clubs." It comes as no surprise that he played his football in midfield, where that ability to pluck high balls out of the sky was fine-tuned.

Comparing a rugby fullback to a GAA midfielder, Kearney says: "They're probably the two most similar positions on both teams. Fielding in both positions is probably the most important attribute you can bring really. I've been practising it from a young age so I'd bloody want to be good at it."

Of course, a crossover between sports can only be of benefit to the sport which a player ultimately specialises in, be it the professionalism and single-minded determination which golf and swimming also fostered in Paul O'Connell, or soccer for the likes of Ronan O'Gara and Jerry Flannery, but Gaelic football is perhaps the closest in terms of its skills' set. "I think evasion is a big part of Gaelic football too," says Kearney, adding: "You've got your support play and probably the biggest thing of all in Gaelic football would be your peripheral vision, and unlike rugby you've got players coming at you from all directions."

Brian O'Driscoll didn't play any rugby until he went to secondary school in Blackrock; Gaelic football was his preferred game until that point. He played in primary school with Belgrove, but predominantly with Clontarf GAA club, and recalls modestly: "Actually, the year after I left to go to Willow in sixth class, they (Belgrove) got to Croker to play in a final. So I was the only one holding them back!"

The Irish captain moved between midfield and the half forward line, and was "a bit of a points scorer, but I suppose I had a bigger engine in those days too.

"I would have played a lot of GAA back in those days, far more than any other game from about the age of seven to 12," he recounts, and has no doubt it helped his rugby. "Definitely in the hand-eye co-ordination. You can see the guys who are good footballers, people like Shaggy (Horgan) and Kearney and Geordan that are so good under the high ball. There are not many sports that you have to catch the ball above your head. So I think it does count for a huge amount and being spatially aware as to getting from point A to B to catch a ball, and to find space."

Given so many of this team and squad have played Gaelic in their formative years it adds to the buzz of representing Ireland at the home of the GAA. O'Driscoll concluded: "I think it gives us a great appreciation for what it means to Ireland as a whole and I think it makes us feel all the more honoured to be allowed play there because we know the history that goes with it. And this is the last time we play England here, so (it's about) enjoying it while we can."

THE GAA INFLUENCE-PLAYER BY PLAYER

ROB KEARNEY

As is abundantly clear from his peerless excellence under the high ball, Kearney played with Cooley Kickhams in Louth all the way through to under-18s and virtually always in midfield. He then played for three years on the Louth minor team, coming within a kick of a Leinster championship final at Croke Park only to be denied by Dublin.

TOMMY BOWE

Played Gaelic football with his local club Emyvale and with the Monaghan under-16s and under-17s. "I only trained with the Monaghan minors, I never actually played for them," he points out.

BRIAN O'DRISCOLL

Played Gaelic football at primary school, Belgrove Boys, and with Clontarf GAA club, combining this with rugby even after going to Blackrock in secondary school, playing a few games up until under-15.

LUKE FITZGERALD

The son of a celebrated former Irish tighthead, Des, combined rugby with football and hurling, playing both codes in his primary school and then with Naomh Olaf until he was 13.

RONAN O'GARA

Combined rugby (with Cork Con), soccer (with Summerstown) and tennis with football and hurling in the Bishopstown GAA Street Leagues and Scoil Spioraid Naomh, continuing with football longer than hurling, which he gave up at about 12, as he was better at football.

TOMÁS O'LEARY

Son of Cork hurling legend Seánie, who was on the Cork Championship team in the 1980's, O'Leary is the most famed GAA player in the Irish squad. He played hurling, football and soccer at St Patrick's Boys School in Gardner's Hill, thereafter combining rugby at CBC Cork with hurling and football with Erin's Owen until he was 19. In his second year on the Cork minor hurling team he captained them to an All Ireland title in 2001 at the age of 17, and then played a year with the county's under-21s, whereupon he was offered a year with the Irish Academy by the IRFU.

MARCUS HORAN

Horan attributes his hand-eye co-ordination to hurling, which he played to intermediate level with Clonlara in the Clare Championship and had trials for his county, but maintains: "I would have been average."

JOHN HAYES

The Bull didn't play his first rugby match until he was 19 prior to which he played Gaelic football and hurling with his local club, Doon CBS, pretty much in every position from the fullback line to the full forward line, though by his own admission wasn't especially good at either.

BRIAN O'DRISCOLL'S QUARTERBACK SNEAK RESULTS IN A TRY AGAINST ENGLAND

DONNCHA O'CALLAGHAN

Played Gaelic football with his club, Bishopstown, from the age of 10 to 15 and although hurling is there now it wasn't then. He and his brothers combined this with rugby. "We used to get brain damage from the coach to 'give a bit to your parish'. We'd have a game for Highfield and then jump over the wall to play a football match, normal stuff for a kid."

DAVID WALLACE

Wallace only played football at lunchtime in Monkstown National School in Cork

JAMIE HEASLIP

Combined rugby and swimming with some Gaelic football on and off with Naas until he was 15, playing in midfield and at full forward though, as he quips, "nothing like big-time Kearney."

JERRY FLANNERY

Starred in goal for St Munchin's.

PAUL O'CONNELL

Played hurling and football from under-8 to under-14 with South Liberties in Limerick, the club whose colours JP McManus's horses run in and a club who backboned the 1973 Limerick All Ireland hurling winning team. A midfielder in hurling and a full forward in football, unlike his rugby, golf and swimming, "I never really excelled".

IRELAND MUST OUTWIT THEM, NOT OUTMUSCLE THEM

28:02:09, CROKE PARK, **LIAM TOLAND**

I'm worried, very worried and I've plenty of cause to be. This England team can beat Ireland. They can do so because they have the ability to dictate the pace of the ball which can neuter the Irish back three and drag us into an ultimate fighting contest. Many lessons have been learned over the months since Declan Kidney and his staff took over. There is a clear style being developed which marries the slow lineout maul with the devastating off-the-top ball. There is a halfback pairing that can share the load of running the match.

You will notice the flow of ball to Ronan O'Gara is no longer as manic as in times past. There is also a back three which, when given the opportunity, can be just as pretty as the fancy French in full flight. Furthermore, there is a scrum that handled both the French and then the mighty Italians: not to mention an outstanding lineout. And finally defensively, this Ireland team is very mean, conceding just two tries in as many matches.

However, the English will have also learned lessons. The level to which the English video nerd can expose Ireland remains to be seen, but we must expect an almighty tussle that will have us very worried. Last March 15th, 2008, I sat in Twickenham watching the English dictate the pace of the ball and destroy Ireland 33-10. Much has happened since but Ireland still remain very vulnerable at the breakdown. On reviewing that match from 12 months ago there were two major factors that can prove fruitful tomorrow.

The first and the positive one was Rob Kearney's outstanding try, the result of brilliant ball carrying, changes of angle and massive ambition. Ireland had a lineout on the English 22 metre line within three minutes of kick-off which found Jamie Heaslip at two (first decoy). Eoin Reddan fired out a long pass to Shane Horgan behind the backs of Denis Leamy and David Wallace (second decoy). Horgan then popped the ball to O'Gara who had a range of options.

Both Andrew Trimble and Tommy Bowe ran very hard into the faces of the England defence (third decoy) but O'Gara launched the ball in front of them to the mercurial Geordan Murphy at fullback, who, by stepping towards the touchline, attracted the last three English outside defenders, Jamie Noon, Iain Balshaw and Paul Sackey. Finally, Kearney stepped off his wing to receive the deftest of passes from Murphy and a hard running angle brought him through Phil Vickery and over the line.

The lesson, much like Brian O'Driscoll's try against the French, was once the ball left hooker Rory Best's hand at the lineout it didn't come into contact with the "enemy" or hit the deck. No breakdown, no ruck and two outstanding tries. By the seventh minute Ireland were on fire and led England by 10 points to nil. The second major factor, the negative, took 70 odd minutes to unfold as England dictated the pace of the breakdown, slowing Ireland's ball to 10 second recycles. In contrast, England could recycle in four seconds, speed up the game, move the Ireland players left and right and, critically, get their big men on the ball. Paul Sackey is a frightening figure and with ball in hand it's a fait accompli.

However, there's major hope for us all and it comes in the strangest of guises. Last weekend I co-commentated on two Magners League matches on Setanta (Glasgow versus Cardiff and Scarlets versus Leinster). Then I watched the Munster versus Edinburgh match, which brought me to Sunday, whereby I was worn out by rugby - and thankfully so.

So to Thurles I went via TG4 and to the club All Ireland semi-final between Ballyhale Shamrocks and Portumna. A majestic game that produced six goals and 27 points, with the Galway club getting through. The shining light by a country mile was Joe Canning, the young Portumna full forward. The range of skills and inventiveness he displayed was mesmerising. So much so that local farmer John O'Grady likened him to a Grand National winner striding proudly, head held high. For a reasonably sized athlete he rarely utilises his bulk, preferring skill, pace of thought and a dexterity that bamboozles his opponents.

He can create space at pace that his teammates consistently exploit. And it is him, or at least his skills that can separate Ireland from England come tomorrow afternoon. Let's face it, the muscle of England, if unfettered, will strangle Ireland. Clearly England have all the power, ability and

ENGLAND'S TOM CROFT CAN'T STOP PAUL O'CONNELL FROM WINNING POSSESSION.

athleticism to spoil the party in Croke Park and unless Ireland mimic Canning and look deep inside themselves and utilise the skills that will outwit Sackey and co, we will lose.

For starters, Luke Fitzgerald must be involved every three minutes. He has to pop up in the strangest of places. Like the inside shoulder of O'Gara and off O'Leary at ruck time. But where Fitzgerald can do most damage is in trailing behind Paul O'Connell and company when they are rampaging down the field; hiding behind the tall trees, if you like, ready to pounce. A roaming role, if you will.

I'm going out on a limb here, I know, but I think Ireland might come unstuck today. And I'll say it once again if Ireland don't win the Grand Slam it will be because we've failed to dictate the pace of the breakdown, allowing England to focus in on our weaknesses and not theirs.

The England selection is telling, with a group of average internationals but excellent club players who lack a world-class leader. They will be compelled to do their master proud. So to their master, the 2003 World Cup-winning captain, 1997 Lions Test series winner, back-to-back European Cup winning captain and a man who claimed five Premiership titles, who now resides at the helm of England and without doubt the greatest bully rugby has ever produced, I give him this: "It's the unconquerable soul of man, not the nature of the weapon he uses, that insures victory" (Gen George S Patton).

I'll be there with my dad so, come on Ireland . . .

MEDIA GIVE JOHNSON RED-CARPET TREATMENT

28:02:09, CROKE PARK, JOHN O'SULLIVAN

The preamble took about 10 minutes. Martin Johnson had fielded questions about penalty counts, South African referee Craig Joubert and the venue for today's Six Nations match, Croke Park; his answers were peppered with an occasional gentle chiding of his inquisitors. The England coach had unfurled himself in a seat that seemed ridiculously small for his frame. He knew the query would come eventually. The moment was flagged by a gentle loosener.

"What's your welcome been like in Dublin?"

Johnson allowed the hint of a smile to cross his lips: "Fantastic."

Really?

"Yeah, very warm, definitely has. (It's) been too friendly, to be honest."

Undaunted an inquisitor persisted. "(A) taxi driver mentioned your reaction in 2003," a reference to the famous red carpet incident when Johnson, then England captain, refused to budge when it was pointed out that the Ireland team traditionally stood on that side of the carpet nearest the Lansdowne Road end.

The culmination of Johnson's refusal to shift was that Ireland marched down past the England team and President Mary McAleese was forced to go off piste to greet the home team. Johnson's first return to Ireland in an official capacity was not going to pass without a reference to "carpet-gate".

The England coach continued: "Nobody's mentioned it so far. I'll let you know when they do."

Persistence is one of the media's many virtues. "Is that still, as you said in your best-selling book, a genuine mistake?"

Johnson: "Is that, did I lie in my book?"

Inquisitor: "No, no, I'm saying, is that still the case? As far as you're concerned, what happened that day was a genuine mistake as opposed to a premeditated plan to upset the Irish?"

"Leave it alone! I told you on Wednesday to leave it alone."

Inquisitor: "You didn't leave it alone in your book, why should I leave it alone?"

"That book was published the same year as the incident, that's six years ago."

Inquisitor: "Yeah, and it's still talked about, England are one of your teams."

"It's talked about mainly here with you guys, not talked about here in Dublin. Things have moved on."

Inquisitor: "People here still talk about it."

"Next question."

Inquisitor: "Genuine mistake?"

"You're asking me, did I lie in my book?"

Inquisitor: "No, I'm not. Do you regret it?"

"I haven't really thought about it."

It should be pointed out that the occasional wry smile was exchanged along with the words. Johnson was much more forthcoming on a variety of other subjects, one of which was Croke Park. The England coach enthused: "Great stadium, fantastic. (It has) a wide surface, bigger than a normal rugby pitch. All the guys who played last time said it was a great atmosphere, despite the scoreline. (We're) looking forward to it."

He was also satisfied that his team have addressed the issues pertaining to penalty count and yellow cards that undermined them against Wales. Johnson has spoken with Joubert, but, more appositely, with his players. "We met the referee yesterday (Thursday), (had) a perfectly good meeting with him and now looking forward to the game. It's just making calls in the heat of the battle. You're always going to get ones that go against you; that you can argue against. That's part of the game.

"It's a difficult area for the referee. We need to do everything in our power to be as clean as we can there. They (the players) can't back off. You've got to make a decision, whether to go in and compete, or not. When they go in and compete, they've got to be accurate and get out if knocked on the floor."

STEPHEN FERRIS AND PADDY WALLACE SANDWICH ENGLAND'S TOBY FLOOD

IRELAND HAVE THE TEMPO TO RAISE SPIRITS

28:02:09, CROKE PARK, GERRY THORNLEY

Once again, a nation not only expects but demands a win in what seems to be the only source of good news around.

And the only source of cash as well. Though English fans appeared to adopt a decidedly low profile two years ago, a survey from that fixture showed that the economic impact for the local economy was in the region of €80-90 million. And, of course, the feel-good factor from a win can scarcely be measured.

Ireland is not unique, and similar noises about lifting the prevailing gloom had been emanating from the Welsh camp - until last night.

But when all this was put in the context of 30 variously shaped men chasing after a pumped up piece of leather as the forecast rain clouds converge on Jones Road, coach Declan Kidney understandably drew a sharp intake of breath. "No pressure then," he said, smiling wryly.

"If we were to say that our desire to win tomorrow was greater than before, that would belie any team that has gone before us," he added. "I think we're very conscious that we're a representative side. We want to do that to the best of our ability.

"Pressure? Not really, I think this is a good place to live. We have a great sporting public in Ireland. People know that once we give it everything we have, they'll go with us. That's where the pressure comes from - to be as good as we can be."

Kidney and captain Brian O'Driscoll cut relaxed figures at their eve-of-match press conference, as did all in the Irish camp later as they mucked around with a Gaelic football on the hallowed turf. If there is pressure there, and from the outside it would appear to be enormous, then, like two years ago, it isn't showing.

Even a question regarding his insight into England coach Martin Johnson drew an Eric Cantona-like pearl from the Irish captain.

"Knowledge is knowing tomato is a fruit; wisdom is knowing not to put it in a fruit salad," said O'Driscoll. Perhaps one he washed and prepared earlier?

As for the pre-match stand-off in 2003, when Johnson refused to swap ends for the presidential greeting, O'Driscoll commented: "It began as an accident but he stood up for what he felt. You have got to respect that."

Indeed the World Cup-winning force of nature demands respect. "He wants to win every place he goes when he's involved in a team," said O'Driscoll. "He'll bring the best out of his team because of that."

Wales' win over England was a reminder of how much the Celts like to beat England, but also perhaps how uncomfortable they are when in the more rarified air of favourites. It also showed that Johnson, one of the shrewdest rugby brains around, is perhaps starting to design a team in his own obdurate image.

Not only did the weight of history bear down heavily on the fixture two years ago, when England appeared to be taking on far more than 15 rugby players, this time the Red Rose will be altogether more settled and better prepared. The return of Joe Worsley has solidified Mike Ford's defence, and this England looks designed to frustrate the home side for long stretches with a relatively structured, spoiling and bruising game.

There's plenty of prime beef in the pack, they have a strong scrum and five big men to launch in the air, including Nick Kennedy, an excellent lineout operator who specialises in nicking opposition ball.

Yet England's confidence must be relatively brittle given five defeats in their last seven Test outings.

As with the win over France, Ireland will require an excellent, all-round team performance to prevail, with Ronan O'Gara a pivotal figure. Though not perceived to be on top of his game in the opening two matches, this is perhaps down to the extra box-kicking load assumed by Tomás O'Leary.

Even so, each time O'Gara came through strongly and the occasion of his 90th Test is primed for him. He is within 11 points of overtaking Jonny Wilkinson's all-time championship record of 479 points, and of reaching 900 Test points.

He may well be asked to play a territorial game, at least early on.

Although England's countering threat would not appear to be in France's league, either way, Ireland's kicking game has to clear England's back three or have enough air to apply more pressure than in the championship opener.

Coupled with pressure on the scoreboard, without a Danny Cipriani-like figure even on their bench, England do not appear well disposed toward playing catch-up.

Alternatively, were they to build a lead it could be a fraught and taut night.

Ireland's accuracy in the setpiece has been a bedrock of the two wins to date. It perhaps faces its toughest test, and Ireland perhaps do not thrive in a war of attrition.

That is England's domain, though the ELVs and the crackdown at the breakdown weren't only with a team in red in mind, but also one in all white. The laws make it harder for a team to stuff the ball up their jumpers or keep it tight with pick-and-go until some bloke called Jonny is worked to within three-point range.

With a pacier, more dynamic backrow, Ireland also look more capable of playing at a higher tempo, of launching O'Driscoll at the English midfield or bringing Rob Kearney into the line from quick-off-the-top ball, or from a few rapid, quick-fire phases.

Therein may lie the key: Ireland's ability to generate quick ball. And it could be that Peter Stringer and Gordon D'Arcy will ultimately play key roles.

You suspect that the team with more variety and tempo to their game, and who are perhaps fractionally more assured in what they are doing, will get there in the end, but it's liable to be a bruiser.

Bring it on, 80 minutes of fun and games.

GRAND DESIGNS COME INTO FOCUS

02:03:09, CROKE PARK, **GERRY THORNLEY**

Dublin was heaving on Saturday night as tens of thousands took the view that a win is always worth celebrating, particularly as an antidote to these recessionary times. And it will be a sad oul'day when we don't celebrate a win over England. Yet, rarely can one recall such contrasting views of what had unfolded. It either bordered on ugly, or was a thunderous and absorbing collision.

Admittedly, the French game a fortnight before had used the full expanse of the pitch, with the aerial ping-pong punctuated by vintage French counter-attacks and Ireland's willingness to run and strike from deep as well. But when the action becomes as concentrated as it did for stretches on Saturday, the exchanges can appear remote. Perhaps too many in the 81,163 attendance were expecting something resembling the wondrous and clinical 43-13 victory of two years before.

The atmosphere crackled at the outset, but thereafter it ebbed and flowed, at times assuming all the fervour of a Leonard Cohen concert, until some English skulduggery or pressure on the English line livened up proceedings. The relief at the end was palpable, all around the ground and on the pitch. It should never have been a one-pointer, and but for Ronan O'Gara's radar going askew it wouldn't have been.

On Saturday evening, one of his former teammates likened him to a thoroughbred horse, ie, one that needs to be finely tuned, but if there's something off-kilter it can upset him more readily than most, and prompt even him to ask himself: "What the **** is going on?"
The irony is that he landed five from five with the Mitre ball in Rome. But let's give the lad a break: he dropped 11 potential points - not 17, as someone on RTÉ was reported to have said - and with 895 points in Test rugby it's not as if he's in debt to his country. O'Gara has bailed Ireland out many times.

Here, Ireland wouldn't have won without Brian O'Driscoll, who now rivals the colossal Paul O'Connell for the Superman garments. Aside from doing his fairly peerless stuff as a number 13, at times O'Driscoll did passable imitations of a seven (those trademark turnovers while playing the ball on his feet) and a 10 (the drop goal), not to mention the perfect body positioning which any prop would have been happy with for his third try in the three games and his 35th for Ireland.

Coach Declan Kidney, always uncomfortable when asked to sing individual praises, highlighted the collective leadership of O'Driscoll, O'Connell and O'Gara, adding: "He's playing well in a team that's going okay. He's playing his part, and that's what he does. It seems with Brian it can be a little bit manic (media coverage): he's way off target one day, and the next . . . (but) it depends on what goes on around you.

"I'd have to say an awful lot for Ronan today. You miss one or two penalties and all of a sudden you can go into your shell. He didn't. When we needed a conversion to put us up, or a penalty, he was the man that stood up. He never shirked it. Today was one of Brian's better days, and I'm delighted for him. But I always look on the fella who's not having a good day, it's how he digs in that could be the

DONNCHA O'CALLAGHAN GETS AIRBORNE IN SUPPORT OF TOMMY BOWE

deciding factor."

The pressure is intensified by a nation which craves the kind of success which this generation of players is good enough to achieve, led as it is by probably the best Irish player of any generation. And, as the prize nears, so the hardest part is still to come, with away trips to Scotland and Wales. "We're having a bit of craic, that's an important part of it," said Kidney. "There's a lot of experience in the team, they've been down different roads before and we want to try and put that to good effect with some of the younger fellas coming in.

"But there's nobody like Scotland to disturb a party. They have a huge pack. I don't know if you saw what the Scottish scrum did to the Italian scrum. It looked to me in the few minutes that I saw that they (the Scots) were more than comfortable. And we would struggle against that Italian scrum and their physicality. We just have to see how it goes, but it's a bit of craic for the next two weeks."

The negatives? "Our understanding of how to speed the game up and recycle the ball against a defence like that, we definitely need to take a look at that," he admitted. "Getting over the gain line on the front (foot) and being able to recycle was very difficult today, and that's certainly something we're going to have to take a look at, because Scotland are every bit as big as England."

Much of the post match debate - and virtually every post match interview by Martin Johnson or his players - focused on England's continuing ill-discipline. Their tally of 10 yellow cards in four games must be unprecedented, and equally costly here was the penalty count of 16-8. "It's very annoying. I've just told the guys that it has cost us a Test match. All that work you put in to try to win a game is gone, wasted," said Johnson, who said he felt "angry for the players. It's not one individual doing it all, it's a number of individuals at key moments."

Yet as befits a team seemingly designed primarily to stop the opposition, collectively they are serial offenders. Ireland are no shrinking violets and have flirted with the offside line, but they don't constantly talk to the referee. England lived offside and "hands away white" could be set to music.

Phil Vickery and Delon Armitage, especially, played on the edge, each cynically slapping the ball from Tomás O'Leary's hands. Mike Tindall and Armitage each blocked Rob Kearney and O'Driscoll off the ball, and Riki Flutey deserves to be cited for his late, high shoulder charge on the Ireland captain. Good bloke and wonderful, on-field force of nature that he was, for all of Johnson's table thumping and handwringing, the old saying comes to mind that a team reflects the personality of its manager. Indeed.

IRELAND CHANGE TACK TO GO THE MUNSTER WAY

02:03:09, CROKE PARK, **GERRY THORNLEY**

IRELAND 14 ENGLAND 13

Anyone expecting a beauty contest would have been disappointed, but they would have been misguided in the first place. This was always likely to be an arm-wrestle. As World Cup opponents can testify, not to mention Wales a fortnight ago, it's the way of things when England take to a rugby pitch, so Ireland can take plenty of satisfaction in taking them on and outmuscling them. England came to Dublin to play cup rugby and Ireland responded in kind. The lines in the sand were drawn, and so intent were both sides on playing territory and building a lead it became a bit like chess.

Ireland did enough to achieve the first part of the game plan except, alas, on the scoreboard, as Ronan O'Gara's missed brace of first-half penalties prevented them from building a 9-0 lead. Instead, they turned around at 3-3, and were making little impression on England's well drilled defence. Joe Worsley was put in at outhalf on Irish scrum ball, with Toby Flood packing down at flanker, to cut down Jamie Heaslip's surges.

And England's destroyer helped flood the midfield, where too much of the onus was placed on Brian O'Driscoll. And, dance as he might, even a vintage O'Driscoll couldn't find space. When O'Gara's radar went awry again, Ireland took to a different route. They had arguably tried to make too many passes and then - as Declan Kidney and the coaches pointed out at half-time - when within 30 metres of the English line, had wrongly gambled on grubbers three times.

So they rolled up their sleeves, took England on closer in, and kept the ball in a Munsteresque change of tack. Rarely has a team worked as hard for a 11-3 lead, courtesy of a sweetly struck drop goal and a close range rumble by the majestic O'Driscoll. But, as much as anything, the decisive third quarter, and indeed the performance overall, was testimony to the improved cohesion of the pack under Gert Smal's direction.

O'Driscoll was still feeling the effects of Riki Flutey's shoulder charge into his jaw and Delon Armitage's late block when his lieutenants opted to go for the corner. Had John Hayes not stumbled from Paul O'Connell's feed he might well have scored from a smartly worked move. That's quite a testimony to their collective confidence in that machine. As it was, three times they went to the corner, and when Phil Vickery was binned for slowing the ball down they cleverly opted for a scrum to force England to withdraw James Haskell.

It was then O'Driscoll muscled over. O'Gara missed the conversion. Had he taken his kicks, Ireland would have been 22-3 up. Not only would we be viewing this performance a whole lot differently, but Ireland would probably have gone on to win comfortably. In any event, they were given another leg up by the kind of crass ill discipline that blights England's efforts when Danny Care lined up Marcus Horan and cynically blindsided him. O'Gara had the courage to nail the match-sealing penalty.

Those who live by the sword. Though Toby Flood and, to his credit, Andy Goode, put some attacking shape on their game, with Flood even working a rare line break by Mathew Tait in the game's best setpiece move, England are a negative, spoiling team. There could have been more yellow cards; cynical blocking, slowing down ball and focusing on stopping the opposition seem part of their DNA. You wouldn't like to watch them every week. They are like a better paid Italy.

The importance of that score was underlined when Goode worked a line break and then had the vision to grubber kick through for Delon Armitage to outrun Horan and make the last minutes a good deal more fraught than they ought to have been. That try brought to mind the Maxime Medard one in the same corner against France, when the French winger was in a footrace with Rory Best to score easily following a Lionel Beauxis kick. The common denominator both times was that Luke Fitzgerald vacated his berth to join a ruck that he had no business joining.

He's a great talent, and it's all in Fitzgerald's praiseworthy work ethic, which, along with his tackling, have been exemplary. And though he was

GIVE US A HUG: JAMIE HEASLIP AND MARCUS HORAN CELEBRATE A THIRD WIN

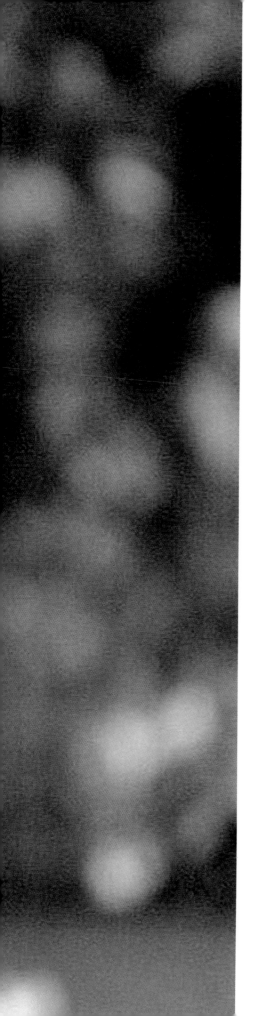

living off scraps, his line onto Tommy Bowe's arcing run infield and typical awareness briefly hinted at the try of the season. But this defensive glitch is something that Les Kiss will seek to iron out between now and Murrayfield. Winning a war doesn't mean you have to die for your country.

Another marked difference is the more aggressive and, hence, offensive defence. Whereas before it was a defence that strove to keep its shape and absorb pressure, Ireland have upped their line speed in more of an "outside-in" banana shape and have entrusted big hitters such as Stephen Ferris, O'Driscoll and Bowe to leave the line and take out ball carriers. It trusts players to make decisions and it's more of a risk, but it's also forcing more turnovers and there were several examples of that here.

On the negative side, O'Gara's kicking and game have become an issue, while Ireland still need to up their offload tally, to generate quicker ruck ball and to create more one-on-ones out wide. Tomás O'Leary played well and his box kicks were much better, but Peter Stringer again upped the tempo. And there seemed a case for introducing Gordon D'Arcy, but O'Driscoll's battle scars probably prevented that. He'll have ached yesterday, but would have felt a good deal worse if Ireland had contrived to lose.

Fortunately, the Irish camp had braced themselves for what to expect from the Red Rose. All part of the Six Nations' rich tapestry.
Sometimes you have to win ugly.

BLOODY-MINDED IRISH WIN BATTLE OF SMALL INCHES

02:03:09, CROKE PARK, **LIAM TOLAND**

As Craig Joubert's whistle blew for the last time and the curtain finally fell on the Croke Park odyssey, a very large English gentleman shook my hand and apologised, whilst stating that "Wales will hammer Ireland". Over my shoulder I heard an Irish man bemoaning a boring match. I couldn't help but ask myself were all these people at the same match? Boring? Ireland will be hammered by Wales?

Maybe I simply adore rugby, but watching old gladiators such as Mike Tindall and Phil Vickery give their all to the English cause was never boring. Watching John Hayes on his 92nd cap battle every inch with the Minotaur, Andrew Sheridan, was never boring. Witnessing Joe Worsley's immense tackle count of 15 bone-crunchers was never boring. Not to mention Brian O'Driscoll's physicality, work-rate and leadership. None of which were boring.

Both teams battled for every available square inch, so much so they replicated American football coach Tony D'Amato's unforgettable words . . . "On this team we fight for that inch, on this team we tear ourselves and everyone else around us to pieces for that inch. We claw our fingernails for that inch, because we know when we add up all those inches, that's going to make the f****** difference between winning and losing, between living and dying."

Yes, Friday night's encounter in Paris was beautiful and entertaining, but it too was a battle of inches and France were not prepared to relinquish one inch to the Grand Slam champions. Like O'Driscoll yesterday, the French centre Yannick Jauzion was immense. And thankfully for us, both France and Stade Francais centre Mathieu Bastareaud are firmly behind us, because the French are back.

As for O'Driscoll, he was simply superb, and why the English persisted in attacking his channel was puzzling. Even in his quieter moments in 2008 his defence has always been unquestionable. England were very naive to think he'd crack. And certainly secondrow Nick Kennedy was, finding himself dumped by O'Driscoll on the 25th minute. Ryan Jones missed the Welsh opener against Scotland and he was anonymous against the French on Friday night. There's no question O'Driscoll is the frontrunner for the 13 slot in South Africa, and with a 10 out of 10 performance on Saturday in all facets of the game, most notably leadership, it will certainly be an Irish Lions' captain.

So where does one start reviewing Ireland's third victory? Let's start with the anthems. I defy any GAA stalwart to point out an occasion in Croke Park's history where the anthem was rendered so clearly, so passionately from beginning to end. As my dad neatly summarised: "That's magic". However, rugby by its nature can make for a poor spectacle. Where a bad match of hurling in Croke Park is still extremely entertaining, in rugby it takes a very patient spectator to appreciate the battle that unfolds, especially when it is as dogged as it was on Saturday. But all over the field there were fascinating subplots.

The lineout provided one, where Paul O'Connell and his lifters once again reigned supreme. A subtle difference in their lineout defence was telling. The English, mainly through 6ft 8in beanpole Kennedy, defended in zones. Banking on the perceived arrival of the ball, they wait, not moving, until inevitably the ball had arrived to a moving O'Connell metres away. Opportunity missed. Ireland, conversely, relied on their ability to move quickly on the ground.

In doing so they demonstrated the greater feeling for the game. Through many hours of preparation under Gert Smal they could rely on the symbiotic relationship between lifter and jumper. This is all very telling, as the Ireland lineout has improved dramatically, allowing O'Connell and co several clean catches and, once again, the platform to attack and defend.

The defence at the tail was also interesting. Joe Worsley, a player I've always struggled to figure out, was incredible. He flew off the tail of the lineout time and again to hoover up space on the inside channel which laid the foundation to England's steely defence. His outside defenders had huge confidence in his ability to police the 10 channel. Several times the tussle between himself and David Wallace at the tail became comical, with trips, flicks and decoys. Both prevented access to the other's outhalf.

England's interpretation of the laws has been suspect since the autumn. But to witness Toby Flood sprinting up to a fallen Rob Kearney was painful. A 10 year old knows the player on the ground must be allowed up off the deck. But what did Flood do? Like so many of his colleagues he saw red and launched himself at the prostrate Kearney. Penalty!

It wasn't the huge penalty count or the double yellow cards that did for England, it was the timing of the indiscretions. Obviously there's no good time to concede 16 penalties, but there are bad times. Each one of England's indiscretions prevented momentum which, combined with their four line breaks, could have reversed the result. England made it to the RWC 2007 final because of their ability to expose their opposition's weaknesses over their own. On Saturday they nearly managed it, but this Ireland side is made of sterner stuff and should be proud of themselves.

As I departed Croke Park, I couldn't help feeling enthused by this most basic of battles fought. It was a fantastic victory for O'Driscoll, Kidney, Croke Park and Ireland. And finally, as I turned onto Clonliffe Road, I couldn't help but chuckle at the lady and two kids squashed into the back seat of the car watching a DVD on the headrest, waiting dutifully for their mighty hunter to return from the big match.

ENGLAND COACH MARTIN JOHNSON IS A PICTURE OF DEJECTION

JOHNSON TAKES CARE TO LAY THE BLAME ON INDISCIPLINE

02:03:09, CROKE PARK, **JOHN O'SULLIVAN**

England coach Martin Johnson was greeted like the pantomime villain when sporadic close-ups of his face appeared on the big screen at Croke Park. Forget the booing, it was the animation and gestures he couldn't mask for a fleeting second or two that offered far more illumination than the measured responses of his post match press conference.

Caught unaware by his big screen cameos he didn't try and mask his gut reaction to one or two instances of England on-pitch indiscipline, striking the desk with a fist and on another occasion glaring at the monitor with an intensity that suggested it was just as well the offender wasn't within his grasp. Twenty minutes after the final whistle, his post match dressingroom dissertation must have had a cathartic effect on his disposition by the time he arrived to face the media. It wasn't that he wouldn't have felt angry, disappointed or frustrated but the emotions were less raw. It was time to circle the chariots.

Johnson wasn't impervious to England's disciplinary peccadilloes but rather than single out individual culprits he chose to focus on collective shortcomings; at least for public consumption. It may still be the early months of a new regime but peeking through his thoughts, it's clear to see one or two players won't make the cut when France arrive in Twickenham in a fortnight. In the last four Test matches 10 England players have received yellow cards - Phil Vickery and Danny Care the latest recipients - a millstone that in combination with a ridiculously high penalty count is effectively denying the team opportunities to win matches.

England may have lost by a point but had Ronan O'Gara displayed his customary accuracy, the match would have panned out differently: the visitors having to take more risks in chasing the game, a tactic that would sit a great deal less comfortably than the defensive solidity and kicking game they pursued for most of the match.

Johnson's overview of the contest was something of a lament to lost opportunity, England undermined by their own hand. "I thought it was a good Test match, real tight, with both teams defensively strong, particularly in the first half. It was a mistake in the kicking game that created an opportunity. We probably let them off the hook three or four times in terms of building pressure in their half: missed kick to touch, lost lineout; penalty at a scrum.

"We didn't have that much pressure (as a result). I thought we handled them defensively pretty well. In the first half, the penalty count wasn't great and it got worse. Ultimately I said to the players after the game, you cost yourself a game. You have to face facts. It was a big effort, they (the team) did things very well at times but ultimately, if you give away 16 penalties you are going to lose. The one that really changed the game was Danny's (Care). It was 11-6 at that point and they made it 14-6 and we had no scrumhalf for 10 minutes. There was an opportunity for us to play for the last 10 minutes with Danny on fresh . . . he hit the back of a ruck from where I saw it."

Unfortunately for Care, Johnson's view may be less charitable when he views the video as the Harlequins scrumhalf was guilty of a crass charge into the back of Marcus Horan. "As I said to him (Care) when you're down in the penalty count that much, the referees and the touch judges are looking at you; and why wouldn't they be? The main focus of this week has been hammering away about not giving away penalties and trusting our defence; being accurate in that area.

"We have done it (given away penalties) again. I am just angry for them, not for me, because they work hard. They have come here against one of the better teams in Europe, a team that can win this championship and gone toe-to-toe for great periods. At times they have been under pressure and we have had them (Ireland) under pressure but ultimately if you are going to give 16 penalties away, you are not going to win. It's not the same person all the time. It is a team-wide thing. It's very frustrating. The scoreline is the game. Ronan (O'Gara) missed some kicks but if he kicks them it changes the dynamic as well. If the game stays tight, it stays tight. We scored right at the end: another two minutes, who knows?

"You saw the atmosphere at the start with the anthems. You are playing in a very volatile, passionate place when you come here. I thought, despite the penalties in the first half, we kept ourselves in the game very well. We handled what they had to throw at us particularly well.

"I thought we defended very well again. That's what makes it all the more frustrating about giving the penalties away; we didn't have to as it's not as if we were getting broken defensively. We have got to believe in ourselves and trust in ourselves. "There are other elements as well, not just the discipline, that need to be improved. There was space wider out for us. The ball could have gone there. Our kicking game wasn't as good as it should have been."

Canvassing the England players unearthed identical key words: frustration, anger, disappointment. Captain Steve Borthwick shrugged: "I thought the referee was left by us with no options but to give penalties against us. I think we gave away penalties that were blatant. The players are the only ones that can remedy this situation. We are responsible for the decisions we make out on the field. The last two weeks we have been very close to winning Test matches against very good opposition away from home and we have lost both of them.

"Ultimately the coaches are the ones that can talk about it but it is the players that have to remedy it. Every one of us is angry. We are angry about ourselves collectively; we are all responsible for this. We are building a great unity within the squad so we are angry that we have let ourselves down."

It is the second match in succession England have recognised their shortcomings but the more pertinent issue is whether they can endorse those words with the requisite action or will they offer the same plaintive cry in two weeks' time?

IRELAND 14-13 ENGLAND

O'Gara pen miss	12:42
O'Gara pen miss	21:57
O'Gara pen	28:53
40:49	Flood pen
H-T	
O'Gara pen miss	0:59
O'Driscoll drop	5:01
O'Driscoll try	20:09
O'Gara con miss	21:51
30:38	Armitage pen
O'Gara pen	38:35
47:58	Armitage try
48:35	Goode con

IRELAND

15 **ROB KEARNEY** (Leinster)
14 **TOMMY BOWE** (Ospreys)
13 **BRIAN O'DRISCOLL** (Leinster, capt)
12 **PADDY WALLACE** (Ulster)
11 **LUKE FITZGERALD** (Leinster)
10 **RONAN O'GARA** (Munster)
9 **TOMÁS O'LEARY** (Munster)
1 **MARCUS HORAN** (Munster)
2 **JERRY FLANNERY** (Munster)
3 **JOHN HAYES** (Munster)
4 **DONNCHA O'CALLAGHAN** (Munster)
5 **PAUL O'CONNELL** (Munster)
6 **STEPHEN FERRIS** (Ulster)
7 **DAVID WALLACE** (Munster)
8 **JAMIE HEASLIP** (Leinster)

ENGLAND

DELON ARMITAGE (London Irish) 15
PAUL SACKEY (Wasps) 14
MIKE TINDALL (Gloucester) 13
RIKI FLUTEY (Wasps) 12
MARK CUETO (Sale) 11
TOBY FLOOD (Leicester) 10
HARRY ELLIS (Leicester) 9
ANDREW SHERIDAN (Sale) 1
LEE MEARS (Bath) 2
PHIL VICKERY (Wasps) 3
STEVE BORTHWICK (Saracens, capt) 4
NICK KENNEDY (London Irish) 5
JAMES HASKELL (Wasps) 6
JOE WORSLEY (Wasps) 7
NICK EASTER (Harlequins) 8

REPLACEMENTS

Peter Stringer (Munster) for O'Leary (66mins)
Rory Best (Ulster) for Flannery (69mins)
Denis Leamy (Munster) for Heaslip (69mins)

NOT USED

Tom Court (Ulster)
Mick O'Driscoll (Munster)
Gordon D'Arcy (Leinster)
Geordan Murphy (Leicester)

REPLACEMENTS

Julian White (Leicester) for Sheridan (76 mins)
Danny Care (Harlequins) for Ellis (57 mins)
Matthew Tait (Sale) for Sackey (58 mins)
Dylan Hartley (Northampton) for Mears (66 mins)
Andy Goode (Brive) for Flood (66 mins)
Tom Croft (Leicester) for Kennedy (69 mins)
Luke Narraway (Gloucester) for Easter (76 mins)

Six Nations Championship: Round 3

	P	W	D	L	F	A	Pts
IRELAND	3	3	0	0	82	43	6
Wales	3	2	0	1	65	49	4
France	3	2	0	1	64	59	4
England	3	1	0	2	64	48	2
Scotland	3	1	0	2	52	54	2
Italy	3	0	0	3	26	100	0

FRANCE 21 WALES 16

SCOTLAND 26 ITALY 6

CrokePark, February 28th, 2009. Attendance: 82,000
Referee Craig Joubert (South Africa)
Touch judge Christophe Berdos (France) P Allan (Scotland)
TMO Giulio de Santis (Italy)

SCOTLAND V IRELAND

MURRAYFIELD, MARCH

RUTHLESS DISPLAY SHOULD SEE OFF SCOTS

14:03:09, MURRAYFIELD, **GERRY THORNLEY**

OPTIMISM is high in the ranks of Irish supporters who have been gradually filling Princes Street - currently one long roadwork as Edinburgh builds a tramline from the city centre to the airport - and beyond. The travelling support will be swelled by Scottish-based ex-pats, for how else can one explain this being Murrayfield's first sell-out of the season? Ireland, it would appear, are a bigger draw than the world champions, the world's number one side and reigning Grand Slam/Six Nations champions, all of whom have come to town before them.

It's easy to forget, of course, that rugby in Scotland is a poor second to football - this weekend also sees Edinburgh and Glasgow derbies - and that traditional capacity crowds for Six Nations games masks the difficulty which, say, clubs like Edinburgh and Glasgow have had in drawing support. As Scottish author Christopher Brookmyre once observed, international matches at Murrayfield are "the biggest private school reunions in the world". But the optimism is not confined to Irish ranks. Scotland are in the position many Celtic teams revel in: underdogs at home against the leaders but refreshed by a win in their last outing. This is right up their street.

This Scottish team have also come on immeasurably from their opening day defeat to Wales, not least because Frank Hadden has sharpened their cutting edge by bringing in the Evans brothers. Max Evans is especially creative with his footwork and clever little kicks, while Thom and in-form fellow winger Simon Danielli give them a finishing edge they haven't had in aeons. Almost as significantly, Euan Murray missed their opening two games, having been instrumental in the huge Scottish scrummaging performances against the All Blacks and the Springboks last autumn.

An immensely strong man, and favourite for the Lions' number three jersey, at a stroke his return saw the pack dissect the renowned Italian scrum. Although Allan Jacobsen has been sidelined on the other side of the scrum, it's still liable to be a potent weapon. And, loosehead apart, the other half-dozen changes since the Welsh opener have probably improved the side. Hugo Southwell has played his way off the team, but Chris Paterson has landed all eight of his kicks as a replacement.

Ireland's discipline has been almost exemplary, with a cumulative penalty count of 44-22 in their favour, whereas the Scots have conceded 33 penalties to 26. But one wonders how long this can last under South African referee Jonathan Kaplan today, and particularly whether he and his touch judges keep an eye on the offside line. As is the way of rugby, this has been a campaign of plagiarising: France learned from England's performance against Wales, and Scotland will take a leaf from the English manual today to defend hard from the outside in to clip the width from Ireland's game.

According to the statistics, the Scots have also completed the most offloads (42) and passes (545), whereas Ireland are bottom of the table in both categories (10 and 380). As coach Declan Kidney observed, Ireland have completed the fewest tackles, though this can be attributed largely to how well they have played and dominated possession.

BRIAN O'DRISCOLL TRIES TO SHAKE OFF SCOTLAND'S MAX EVANS

The defence has been excellent, with the "shooters" choosing their moments right and only once let down inside. But they will need to up their double-tackles to cut down on those offloads. The key though, as usual, will be how much hard yards and go-forward ball the Irish pack generate. The weight of expectation rests mostly on Ireland's shoulders, who stand 80 minutes away from a shot at immortality; so this is a huge test for this team and management. It's liable to be a much tougher game than many expect. The scrum may wobble but should survive, while a ruthless and disciplined performance will be necessary as ever against the Scots, particularly in the clear outs.

This is all about Paul O'Connell and co in a mean looking back five matching the forward intensity of the second half against England. Ronan O'Gara's form has been a concern, but he's due a big game today, and being in harness once again with Peter Stringer ought to give him more room and time for decision-making. Ireland will be wary of letting play become a little skittish, with skirmishes rather than trench warfare. But at the same time, if the pack begin to rumble forward and put the Scots on the back foot, they have the strike power to use selectively, particularly with the higher tempo Stringer can inject into the game and with Gordon D'Arcy back alongside the rejuvenated Brian O'Driscoll.

Concerned by the vast amount of insider knowledge in the Scottish camp, the shuffle in personnel may have partly been to make them a little more difficult for their hosts to analyse. But thus far, in three markedly contrasting games, Ireland have also shown the kind of tactical flexibility required in the unique melting pot that is the Six Nations. The Scots also probably nourished the hope that Ireland might be a little overconfident, but the experience of the entire group, plus those four changes, ought to militate against that.

The Scots will have their moments and spells, but Ireland look the better group of players, with a superior all-round game and look more likely to sustain the quality of their performance.

SAY IT: THE GRAND SLAM IS ON THE TABLE

16:03:09, MURRAYFIELD, **GERRY THORNLEY**

YOU ALWAYS sensed it would come down to this. The last game of the championship, at 5.30pm in the Millennium Stadium next Saturday, will pretty much see the whole shooting gallery up for grabs. It can be said now. The Grand Slam is on the table. For Ireland it is a tilt at only their second Slam in history and the first in 61 years, but it comes against the 10-time and reigning Grand Slam champions, who still have their Six Nations title and the Triple Crown to defend and in their 72,500-capacity ground to boot. Oh yeah, there's maybe a few Lions spots up for grabs, and the captaincy as well.

You'd imagine they'll be up for it too, then, probably more so than in any game in this championship to date. Presumably Warren Gatland will pick his first choice team. The rest have been relegated to the supporting cast on the last weekend of the championship after France's challenge faded meekly in an abysmal, embarrassing performance yesterday at Twickenham, where they were routed 34-10 by England. Only Wales can therefore deny Ireland a first title since 1985, but to do so the Red Dragonhood must win next Saturday by at least 13 points.

Gatland and the Welsh management must now be wondering if they made the right call in tinkering so much with their team against Italy, for the permutations now raise the possibility that Saturday's winners will have the booby prize of a Crown and the losers will be presented with the trophy. Remember England's hollow ceremony after being beaten in Dublin in 2001? Ireland will want the whole booty and nothing but the whole booty now. They've earned themselves this shot at immortality.

A 61-year hiatus is a rather long one, but as for the accompanying hype, Ireland coach Declan Kidney said: "That's just what it is. It's the same group of players for the last number of years. They have given huge service to Ireland. I have no doubt that we'll go out and give it a go, whether that will be good enough or not . . . But I think that the genuine sports person, that's what they'll ask of the team and that's what we'll ask of ourselves, and if that's good enough it's good enough, and if it's not we shouldn't cry over spilt milk. We've managed to give ourselves a chance, that's all." Nor was he inclined to shield the players from the country's craving for some good news. "I wouldn't do that, this is a week to be enjoyed, and if you don't enjoy weeks like this you'll never enjoy it."

Once again Ireland's 22-15 win over Scotland on Saturday was no beauty contest, but instead another arm wrestle, and referee Jonathan Kaplan was centre stage for far too much of it. Memo to IRB: punters don't shell out wanga to watch a pedantic lesson in the laws of the game. The huge Green Army can't have especially enjoyed it, but, having made the effort and incurred the cost of travelling to Murrayfield from whatever direction, they made sure they were going to enjoy themselves. Hence, they wore more green and sang louder than the home crowd, especially in the second half.

Half-time, Kidney admitted, "came at a good time for us" after the try-saving tackles by Tommy Bowe and Brian O'Driscoll which prevented the Scots going into the break 10 points up and with their tails up. Championship minutes, and championship moments perhaps? Kidney also reminded us of the late, firsthalf penalty try by the All Blacks which killed off Ireland's challenge last November. "It was pretty calm," Kidney said of the dressingroom at the interval. "They come in and sit down, we have a cup of tea and then we try and get a few messages across. There's no point ranting and raving, they're pros. You try and make your points and the boys take them on board. But is it what you say or is it just that we played a bit smarter? I think it's a whole host of things, so it's not about trying to grab a bit of limelight by claiming it was anything that was said."

Smarter and, as they discussed, with much more intensity, as they retained the ball better and put some pace on it. There were, for the fourth time running, big games from the team's leading men - O'Driscoll and Paul O'Connell - while Ronan O'Gara came through strongly in the second half, and his 17-point haul meant he overtook Jonny Wilkinson as the championship's all-time leading points scorer and Michael Lynagh as the fifth highest points scorer in Test rugby on 912.

JAMIE HEASLIP INDULGES IN A LITTLE PRE-TRY CELEBRATION AGAINST SCOTLAND

The sight of the immense Stephen Ferris pumping his legs late in the game when, by rights, he should have been waning, is typical of the way this team gradually pushes its way to the winning line, work ethic being the team's byword. They are a Munsteresque, pragmatic side. Winning comes before artistic impression. Less can be more. Whatever it takes. Last Saturday had strong echoes of the way they outmuscled England, right down to the time of the breakthrough try at the end of the third quarter.

But they might well need something more than that in the Cardiff shoot-out, and like all the best shoot-outs neither team would have been terribly surprised that it is the other who stands in their way this weekend, although Kidney didn't expect Ireland to be four wins from four at this juncture. Why? "Because I thought the confidence of the team in November wasn't great. And we've talked about the bit of honesty at Christmas. We got a bit of go against France. Eddie (O'Sullivan) was always talking about a bit of momentum; that seems to be backing us up.

"But there's handier ones than having to go to Cardiff and beat Wales," he said with deliberate understatement. "I'll be accused of mind games, but they are Grand Slam champions, they're playing at home, they're playing for the championship, they're playing for the Triple Crown and they rested most of their players this week. Anything else?"

Ireland will need to start with greater intensity than they did on Saturday, and will need more tempo, width and ambition. If they do, then impossible is nothing.

IRELAND TAKE TIME TO STEADY THE SHIP

16:03:09, MURRAYFIELD, **GERRY THORNLEY**

SCOTLAND 15 IRELAND 22

It doesn't get any easier, does it? Unsurprisingly, the Scots were in the mood to spoil the party and up for it big time in what was another taut, fraught, emotionally exhausting affair. And the players must have been pretty drained too. By all accounts they were shattered by the end of it. Such is the way of modern day rugby that there were times on Saturday you watched Ireland go through phase after punishing phase, only to see the Scots strung out across the pitch with numbers aplenty. Pitches look overcrowded and Murrayfield was no different. Games such as this one look like 20-a-side.

Ireland were far from their best in the first half, and seemed almost too constrained and respectful of Scotland for their own good. Either the weight of expectations had overburdened them or they were simply a little nervous, but in truth they were clinging on a fair bit. Perhaps too they were rattled as much by referee Jonathan Kaplan as the Scots, or the ghosts of the past as yet again a referee's decisions and interpretations were the dominant theme of the first 40 minutes particularly.

Previously the most disciplined side in the tournament, not for the first time in an often edgy relationship dating back to when Kaplan controversially refereed a 12-6 win by Western Province in Cape Town 11 years ago, Ireland fell foul of the South African official. Seven of the 12 penalties they conceded here came in that first period. "Ref links" are almost compulsory in this tournament, and it was striking how often Kaplan engaged the voluble Mike Blair or other Scots in explaining some of his decisions whereas the one time an Irish player dared to speak - Brian O'Driscoll even beginning his response by saying 'sir' - he was given short shrift.

The Ireland captain had been penalised for seemingly trying to free ruck ball with his right foot three times. As with another couple of Chris Paterson three-pointers for scrum infringements, it was reasonable to wonder whether another referee would have made the same calls. It allowed the unerring Paterson to keep his side in front, though it could have been worse. Ronan O'Gara was playing quite deeply, and the Scots' line speed in defence was noticeably quicker, whereas Ireland were unusually softer in midfield and out wide.

All of this contributed to the Scots winning the collisions as Graeme Morrison made too many yards for comfort up the middle and from there they went wide, where the Evans brothers and Simon Danielli had their moments. The Scots' scrum was on top, though they conceded a few indirect penalties for their binding from which Denis Leamy rumbled. T.he home side had 61 per cent of their territory.

The two teams had markedly contrasting restart games. Scotland invariably kicked long for Ireland to concede the throw around halfway - Peter Stringer's box kicking has possibly never been better in his 88 Tests. This contributed to the Scots having eight of the 10 first-half lineouts, but Ireland achieved greater joy from Ronan O'Gara's hanging restarts, reclaiming four of them for valuable possession, territory and points.

Had David Wallace not collared Thom Evans to stop a break out, with only Rory Best on the flanker's outside, or had Tommy Bowe and O'Driscoll not made those try saving covering tackles on the Scottish winger and Phil Godman, the Scots would have been 10 points ahead at the break. Ireland needed the interval more than the Scots, not that they appeared to have seriously doubted their ability to see themselves through this minor little crisis. During it they resolved to up their intensity significantly. O'Gara and Gordon D'Arcy led the line, up in defence, much harder and the outhalf also took the ball flatter as Stringer zipped the ball out. Most of all, their clearouts were much more clinical and Paul O'Connell and co were making inroads into the Scottish lineout as they dominated the territory.

There was an inevitability about the match-turning Ireland try that followed, if less so about its origins. Ireland were going through the phases and Scotland were relying on their stealthy steals but were also now conceding lineouts. From Jamie Heaslip's ball off the top, Peter Stringer spotted John Barclay drifting on to O'Gara and sniped through the gap, eluding Nathan Hines, who had only just come on and was standing in at scrumhalf as Mike Blair adopted a deep, defensive position.

The Irish number nine showed incredible presence of mind and footwork to stand up Blair, buying some time in the process, and swivel and offload for Heaslip to score, as Declan Kidney put it, "eventually". As the coach also pointed out, had Heaslip not grounded the ball properly he would have had some explaining to do to his 14 teammates. Though his exuberance at scoring was entirely understandable, one ventures that Heaslip will be slagged unmercifully by those teammates for showboating and waving to the crowd before touching the ball down one-handed, and that, eh, he won't be doing it again.

 But with that the huge Ireland crowd and team alike could breathe a little easier. O'Gara landed a sweetly struck drop goal and showed remarkable nerve to take on and land a difficult angled penalty to restore Ireland's seven-point lead. It was disappointing that they didn't push on and win a little more clinically and comfortably. Even so, when it came down to the last five minutes, Ireland showed composure and control in abundance to close the game out with a minimum of fuss.

FIRED-UP STRINGER SETS SIGHTS ON NEXT STEP

16:03:09, MURRAYFIELD, JOHN O'SULLIVAN

IN SPORT as in life, having something that is held dear snatched away is a jolt to the senses. There are two ways of responding, bemoaning fate or seeking to react in a positive vein and working harder. Peter Stringer chose the latter. Having been a focal point of scores of Ireland teams he'd nothing to prove in the Test arena only to himself.

He wasn't prepared to let his career taper off, not content to languish on the outside looking in. Restored to first the squad and then the team for Saturday's game he responded with a performance that was adjudged to be of man-of-the-match calibre. He took his chance. It wasn't an 80-minute fanfare but when his pack afforded him a little protection and front foot ball, primarily in the second half, he invited halfback partner Ronan O'Gara out of the pocket and into the front line.

Suddenly the Ireland backline was taking the ball to the right side of the gain line, putting pace and width on the game. There was also the small matter of the break for the only try of the match. Stringer downplayed his role. "Paulie (O'Connell) went up for a ball and their pod matched him (actually Jamie Heaslip won the lineout at the tail). They (Scots) just had one tail-gunner and I was keeping an eye on that as the ball was throw in. Thankfully he shot off and there was a bit of a gap.

"Jamie (Heaslip) was roaring at me from about 15 yards away and thankfully he was there on my inside to finish it off. You know the support is going to get to you. You try and buy as bit of time and keep the defenders guessing. "I heard him (Heaslip) from a good bit away and I just tried to buy a bit of time and draw the defence. The line I took was close to the forwards; I knew if he (Heaslip) wasn't involved in (winning) the lineout he'd be running a support line." Heaslip managed to achieve both remits.

There was an earthy pragmatism to Stringer's post-match comments, a measured delivery that acknowledged the flaws of a patchy collective performance. "We were delighted with the victory but our initial reaction was that we didn't play as well as we had hoped. You have to give Scotland credit for coming out of the blocks in those first 20 minutes; they had a lot of the ball and we were struggling to get hold of it.

"Once we reflected on that and got our scores, it is a bit more satisfying but there are areas to work on for next week. We will go through the analysis a lot more because it can be difficult to take it in immediately after a game. "We started quickly in the campaign and wanted to build on that but as the competition goes on teams analyse you a lot more. Scotland did their homework and we found it difficult to break them down. That's part of the Six Nations, the high intensity games and the analysis that goes into it; when it comes to the end of the championship you are looking for other options and alternatives."

Inevitably Stringer is invited to look forward rather than back and offer his thoughts on a potential "Grand" occasion in Cardiff on Saturday. "It is a massive occasion playing the Grand Slam champions in their own backyard. We set our goals at the start of each campaign. A Grand Slam or a championship is something we want to win. We have been fortunate enough to come away with a couple of Triple Crowns and that's a good

IRELAND'S MAN OF THE MATCH PETER STRINGER FIRES THE BALL AWAY

stepping stone for this even though this (Wales game) is another step up.

"The last couple of weeks we have put in some good performances and some not so good but it is about grinding out victories at times. There is good professionalism in this team, guys are willing to work hard for each other and I'm sure that will be no different at the weekend. Our main focus (as players) will be to concentrate on the job in hand, on our patterns and gameplans and implement them in an arena that's going to be fairly noisy. You have to remain cool headed to bring the best out and that's our challenge both on the day and in the buildup."

Singled out as an individual for his performance, Stringer takes time to highlight the input of the backroom team, name-checking the contributions of coach Declan Kidney and his assistants, Gert Smal, Alan Gaffney and Les Kiss. There is an especially warm mention for the work of analyst Mervyn Murphy. Ireland have reached this stage of the season as a group and now is not the time to break ranks with the ultimate prize tantalisingly close.

FERRIS RELISHES RECALL OF EARLY POSITIVE IMPACT

16:03:09, MURRAYFIELD, **JOHN O'SULLIVAN**

THE MATCH was only seconds old when Stephen Ferris spotted his quarry, calibrated the point of impact and launched himself with a shuddering ferocity. Scotland's number eight Simon Taylor bore the brunt of the impact as best he could manage but was nevertheless tossed backwards with a violence and velocity that drew an audible gasp from the crowd.

Ferris craves opportunities to impose his physicality, a remit he fulfilled with due diligence for 80 minutes at Murrayfield on Saturday evening. Ireland's blindside flanker had a magnificent game from the moment he dumped Taylor to the muddy turf to watching him carry three would-be Scottish assailants on his back 78 minutes later towards their own posts. Constructive and destructive with equal facility, the Ulsterman demonstrated tremendous conditioning to maintain that level of input. It was only when patiently awaiting the end of Declan Kidney's formal press conference that Ferris showed any sign of fatigue, reaching quietly for a chair upon which to plonk his frame.

Victory offered a short-lived balm to soothe bruises and aching limbs but the collisions will leave a legacy for a day or two. Ferris's face brightens at the mention of the Taylor moment as he spools through the memory. "I just knew running up he (Taylor) probably wasn't going to pass it. I wouldn't have in the same circumstances. It's about getting yourself into the game. I was 100 per cent sure that in the first minute he was not going to pass the ball. I just lined him up nicely and put in a bit of an impact. It was good to get that hit on him. It's definitely something I like to do, get a positive moment in a game early on.

"It happened to be in the first minute but you are looking for that in the first five, 10 minutes. It does give you a bit of a lift. I go looking for it in the first few minutes, even if it is carrying (ball) a few yards and offloading. It gives you confidence. I then just went about my job. I thought me, Wally (David Wallace), Jamie (Heaslip) and Denis (Leamy) played pretty well as a unit." It's a fair comment but in the context of the Irish pack, it was post interval that they offered a truer testament of the collective ability. Prior to the interval they were limited to individual cameos, frustrated by slow ball and perplexed by the interpretation of referee Jonathan Kaplan at scrum time.

Ireland's hooker Rory Best admitted: "It (the scrum) was messy as both teams were trying to get the upper hand early on. They have a very good scrum but we'll probably come away with it a little disappointed in terms of the way we did: certainly at the start and end (of the match). The middle bit was all right, we held our own but certainly in terms of where we want to go to, we are a little disappointed." He explained the difference pre and post interval in terms of the team's performance. "They (Scotland) did a great job at our breakdown. We couldn't really get the continuity we wanted in the first half. There were a lot of penalties from our boys as a result of getting isolated.

"In fairness to them, they were in very quickly. I suppose we couldn't get the gain line, which is why we couldn't get any quick ball and because of that we couldn't get the width we wanted. That was probably the big difference between the first half and the first 15 minutes of the second half. We got our gain lines, we got our front foot ball, we got a bit of quick ball and were able to play. That definitely was the winning of the game, the first 15 (minutes) in the second half."

The by-product of a fourth victory is Saturday's Grand Slam collision with the last team to achieve that in the Six Nations, Wales. The players know that the hype will be stratospheric. Ferris smiled: "I will try and distance myself as much as possible from you guys (media), from that side of it (the hoopla) and keep myself focused, mentally and physically prepared. It's going to be a massive encounter.. I'll look for a bit of quiet time, a bit of me time over the next couple of days. Then we'll get down to the hard work that will keep the momentum going. We just need to keep working on everything that we have been doing over the last four or five weeks. There's been so much put into it and to let it all slip on Saturday would be very disappointing. We are going to keep going. We played some good rugby in patches and we will look to add onto that and bring it to Wales."

Best concurred: "When you play any sport, you want to win things. Through a lot of hard work throughout the season we have put ourselves in a position where we can. It is something that we all crave. It's all on the line next week, Triple Crown, Grand Slam, Six Nations Championship. It's exactly where we want to be. If you were told prior to the start of the championship you'd be four from four going into the last weekend, then you couldn't ask for more." Well maybe a fifth win.

THE PEERLESS JACK KYLE

A PITCH-PERFECT ATTITUDE TO LIFE

JACK KYLE WITH SHANE HEGARTY

It is a beautiful day; a beautiful corner of the world. Bryansford sits at the foot of the Mourne mountains, a couple of miles outside Newcastle, Co Down. A narrow road of a village, officially it has a population of 391 people, but does a good impression of a place only half that busy. Today, with spring bringing a little warmth, the mountains are smudged by haze and the road is quiet. Jack Kyle lives just off it, in a small development, almost empty of cars. The address is 13, but the house numbers end at 12.

I call to one for directions. "Number 13 . . . "ponders the occupant. "Jack Kyle's house," I prompt. "Who?" Kyle's house is tucked away, the driveway curving past a small brook that's straddled by a miniature bridge. The steps to the front door are flanked by a white handrail, but as soon as he comes to the door it's clear that he is in fine health. He is 83 now, one of the six surviving Irish Grand Slam winners from 1948, once the most-capped player in the world, declared the greatest Irish rugby player of all time, and described as the finest outhalf by most who saw or played alongside him.

The sports writer Frank Keating saw him play twice, and still believes him to be unsurpassed. On Kyle's 80th birthday he wrote of "the preeminent majesty of freckled, gingery-haired Jack in his old brown boots: patient, calming, unbothered serenity, a pass here, a kick there. Till, in a sudden blur of intensity, a dip of the hip, a glinting change of pace - a trout in a pool - and the game has been snapped open and free with defenders sprawled, rooted as trees." Who, indeed.

Not that Kyle would ever be so self-laudatory. People talk of his humility with as much awe as they talk of his talent. Of course, they are in awe of his humility because of his talent. He soared, but his feet never left the ground. Kyle retired to Bryansford in 2000, returning home after three and half decades in Zambia. He had never emigrated, he says. He was planning his return even as he carved out his life there far from Ireland, so far from news of home that for a couple of decades he rarely saw a rugby match. And when he saw this house - private, quiet, a view of stone-walled fields rising gently away from the back garden - he knew that this was where he wanted to retire to.

It is here that we sit, in the sun room, half facing towards that view, the only noise coming from the chirp of finches crowding the bird feeder. And from the regular interruption of the phone. There are five calls during our conversation. Six if you count one that stops mid-ring. Jack Kyle reacts to each with polite irritation. "Oh, for God's . . . " He pushes himself out of the seat, just a touch gingerly, leaves the heavy heat of the room and walks to the phone. "Hello . . . aye . . . yes . . . well, let's see . . . " Four of the calls are from the press: Reuters, UTV, BBC Radio 4 and a return call from one of those confirming some details. The final time ("Oh, for . . . ") it is his son calling from Kildare, to see how he is, to talk about the trip they'll be taking to Cardiff today. Jack explains that he'll need to do a radio interview over the phone before they leave for the airport. He signs off. "Okay . . . bye now . . . lots of love . . .

When he returned to Ireland, retiring from his career as a doctor, divorced many years ago, his son and daughter had been a little concerned. "One of the interesting things about being away for so long - I was away for 34-and-a-half years and I was working full-time until I was 74 - is that when I came home the kids were thinking 'what's going to happen to dear old dad? He's been away and he's lost contact with a lot of his friends' and so on. But it was amazing to come back and take up with old friends as if I hadn't been away."

There are occasional gatherings of former internationals. Sir Anthony O'Reilly brought a group of former players to Paris for the World Cup final in 2007. He visits his friend and former teammate Jim McCarthy at his Lahinch holiday home. Queen's University has a rugby bursary in his name. He plays golf at Royal County Down every Tuesday, with the "old guys, they call us the Teddy Bears". They play for a pound a game. It is hotly contested. "And the kids thought I was going to be on my own. They thought I was going to be a pain in the neck." He chuckles. "Now it's almost the opposite. 'Dad, how about coming to see us sometime?'"

This week, he should have hired a publicity agent. In 2003, the last time Ireland went into a Grand Slam showdown, he was sought after, but not to this extent. Perhaps it's because of his appearance alongside the RTÉ panel following the English match, when the delighted grins on Hook, Pope, O'Shea and McGurk were brighter than the Croke Park lights. If younger viewers had little idea of who this old guy was, the panel's valedictory applause would have woken them up to his stature.

The house would give you little idea. There's a framed cap marking his induction into the International Rugby Board's Hall of Fame, but a house fire 30 years ago destroyed his memorabilia. He doesn't mind talking about the old days. He would dearly love if this generation had their chance to silence his phone in future years, but "it's pleasant for us to reminisce in a way. And you find yourself sometimes discussing things with people that you wouldn't normally discuss or think about." He sits up a bit. "And can you imagine in your old age if you were sitting here wondering if somebody's going to call and what am I going to do."

He has travelled to the home games in recent years. Surely it takes him an age to get through the handshakes and to his seat. "Well, you know, sometimes you wear your specs and grey hair. People who remember your playing days don't remember you with grey hair. They're probably not expecting it."

He will be in Cardiff today, on a private trip, leaving this morning, returning after the match. In and out in a day. "It's amazing to think that in the 1948 year, our first match was against France and it was on New Year's Day. And, you know, when you think of the travel. Those of us from the North travelled down to Dublin. I think we got the boat across the Irish Sea. Then the next morning we trained in London, stayed in London that night, then the next day took the train to Dover and a boat across the channel to Calais and then a train to Paris. The night before the game I think we were taken out to the Follies Bergère. That was our training for the next day's game."

In Paris, the banquets offered six different glasses, wines for every course. And when the waiter would come along with some delightful bottle dusted off especially for the occasion, Kyle and other teetotal players would ask for an orange juice. He enjoys a glass of wine every evening now, so laughs at the memory of the waiter scooting away, shaking his head, muttering something thoroughly French and thoroughly disdainful.

Then, a rugby tour doubled as an astounding global adventure. In 1950, Kyle went to the southern hemisphere with the Lions. Thirty players. Two managers. One reporter who lasted a matter of weeks before homesickness defeated him. The tour lasted more than six months. At one point, they were a straight two weeks at sea. "Liverpool, across the Atlantic, through the Panama canal, to Hawaii took about a month . . . On to New Zealand, and three months travelling it by bus and train . . . Then a ship across the Tasman Sea to Sydney and a month in Australia . . . On to Sri Lanka or Ceylon as it was in those days . . . back home through the Red Sea and the Suez Canal, via various ports including Marseille and Aden . . . " And what he doesn't mention as he details the trip is that he left the southern hemisphere having been acclaimed as one of the greats of world rugby.

He was born in Belfast in 1926, discovered rugby at school, and entered medicine after the encouragement of his father, who recognised that he was a "dopey sort of kid" not cut out for the business world. "My father was a man of energy and getting things done and I was sort of a bit of a dozer; things happened to me rather than making them happen. I remember my father saying to me one time, 'you'd be dead if you had the sense to stiffen.'"

Even as he began playing at international level - unofficially in 1945 against the British Army, but earning his first of 46 official caps in 1947 - it was always a sideline. He had a single training session a week. The international team would meet on the Friday before a match for a quick run around. Game over, they'd head their separate ways, back to their lives.

"Rugby was part of our lives but it wasn't a big part. It was wonderful to have, but it was a sideline compared with our main aim. Those of us in the amateur era were fortunate that we had careers because if you had a bad game or lost a game, as we did on many occasions, I would be in lectures again on a Monday morning with an exam coming up in a month or two; it certainly concentrated your mind away from having a bad game on a Saturday.

"And when I think of the chaps today and what they have as far as coaching is concerned, looking at videos and being told what they should have done and shouldn't have done, we had nothing like that at all. There were no checks in terms of whether 'you should have passed there and should have kicked there'. So it was very free and easy. So that naturally didn't keep the game in our mind, because it wasn't being talked about as much."

He credits his natural sporting talent to the genetic alchemy created between his parents. His brother played rugby for Ulster and his sisters were fine hockey players, with Betty one of Ireland's greats. But his parents played no sport beyond his father's few games of soccer with a defunct team, the Black Diamonds, in a minor league. "In many ways for me it was almost a humbling experience. That isn't quite the right word, but when somebody says 'how did you score that try?' all you can say is 'I haven't a clue. A gap appeared.' Or 'I got the ball and I started running and other gaps appeared and I got through them.' I don't know how I did it. You're not working at a conscious level. You're at a low subconscious level where there is basic instinct or whatever it is.

"And there were times - and perhaps this is a very corny saying but there's an element of truth in it - sometimes people say you weren't so much playing the game but that the game was being played through you. In other words you were just a vehicle there and you were fortunate that you did the things that enhanced your rugby prowess as well. You realised you were able to do these things just because you were born with the ability. Many a time I've made the analogy that it's like a woman who wants to become a model. She's got to be a certain height and a certain figure and have certain looks before she walks the old catwalk.

"And that's why in many ways you cannot all the time talk about 'I did this' or 'I did that'. I did it but I don't know how I did it. In fact, someone said to me recently 'what initials would you like after your name? Would you like an OBE or an FRCS [Fellowship of the Royal College of Surgeons]?' I said, 'Don't mention the OBE because I did nothing really for that. The FRCS I had to study and work for so if you must put any initials use them because I had to grind those out with my head down.' And sometimes you feel that by sort of saying this that it's false modesty or something like this. It's not. It's just the way I feel. This is the way I was able to play, I don't know whether other good players feel the same way."

Of course, he adds, there were 14 other players on the team, and the forwards did all the grind for his moments of glory anyway. Besides, he insists that his achievements have gathered a little exaggeration along the way. "I only dropped one goal in my life and it was against Wales and it was from the 25-yard line. But people say, 'God that was a wonderful goal you must have been near the 10-yard line'. I don't like to contradict them." In the version I'd been told, he'd kicked the drop goal from the sideline.

He last played international rugby in 1958, and having trained as a surgeon he spent a couple of years working in Indonesia before returning home again for a year. Colleagues told him he needed to "get on the ladder" in the hospitals, but he wanted to go abroad again, just not somewhere cosy or familiar. He took a job in Zambia, a country where few knew about his rugby career, and fewer cared. "There's no use when you're operating on someone telling them, 'by the way do you know how many caps I got?' They're not interested."

In Zambia he was for a time "the only surgeon in this town. And the only surgeon in the next town." The hospital was busy enough that people slept between the beds. Surgery was hair-raisingly varied. "You might have an operating list in which you had to do a burr hole in somebody's skull for a brain haemorrhage and then you might have been operating on the abdomen and maybe operating on a big toe. So I was, I suppose, what the old surgeons in Ireland were 80 or 90 years ago, down the country, turning their hands to anything. It was a really interesting and fascinating life. Naturally, sometimes you felt worse about it, that you would have liked to have expertise in a field. But I suppose there was a consoling factor in a way in that if you didn't do it, no one else was there to do it."

He performed his last surgery less than a decade ago. More recently, he has been a patient. "Ach, I don't . . . I don't want to talk too much about my illness . . ." Last March he discovered that he had a bone marrow tumour but a lot of people, he insists, have suffered a lot worse. The treatment at Belfast City Hospital was "wonderful"; the drug they treated him with, a scientific wonder. It takes a little coaxing to learn from him that during the treatment he developed a back problem and was in hospital for "three or four months", having to learn how to walk again as a result.

He refuses to wallow in it. "I'm now 83. When you're this age, we all have the optimistic attitude like the guy who said, 'I know everyone's going to die but I was hoping an exception was going to be made in my case.'" He laughs. "We realise, I'm afraid, that there are no exceptions. But those of us who have reached this stage, I've had a good life, a very fulfilling life, and I've got to be very grateful and consequently I have to say how fortunate I am to have had these bonus years. I've had more time even after I've been ill. You know I think there's a certain acceptance at this stage that time is running out, so, you know, enjoy it, make the best of it while you can. And this is what one hopes to do."

He grins as he quotes WB Yeats. "When you are old and grey and full of sleep/And nodding by the fire . . ." He has had a lifetime love of reading. There are classical albums and CDs under the window, but the sill is busy with books brought to him during his illness: guides to birds, illustrated artists' biographies, Tim Butcher's Blood River, Graham Swift's Waterland, Mohsin Hamid's The Reluctant Fundamentalist, an autobiography by former Munster captain Anthony Foley.

He prefers nonfiction to fiction these days and has just finished Máire Mhac an tSaoi's memoir out of a curiosity with her husband Conor Cruise O'Brien, whom Kyle met and was greatly impressed by. He also watches the History Channel, especially a current series on great battles. "You know, to keep the neurons firing." He

keeps his French in good condition by watching Euronews en Français. But he retains a special love for poetry, especially Yeats. "I often think of what he wrote in Lissadell. 'The light of evening, Lissadell/Great windows open to the south/Two girls in silk kimonos, both/ Beautiful, one a gazelle . . . '"

Kyle lets the words sit for a moment. Continues. "'Many a time I think to seek/One or the other out and speak/Of that old Georgian mansion,/mix pictures of the mind, recall/That table and the talk of youth,/Two girls in silk kimonos, both/Beautiful, one a gazelle.'"

It is quiet. The phone, thankfully, has stopped ringing for a few minutes. Kyle looks out at the view. It is a glorious day.

PAUL O'CONNELL DROPS HIS SHOULDER AS SCOTLAND'S JOHN BARLAY CLOSES IN

SCOTLAND 15-22 IRELAND

Paterson pen	2:16	
	15:41	O'Gara pen
Paterson pen	14:04	
Paterson pen	21:51	
	28:3	O'Gara pen
Paterson pen	35:18	
	36:52	O'Gara pen
	H-T	
	10:5	Heaslip try
	12:35	O'Gara con
	18:07	O'Gara drop goal
Paterson pen	23:46	
	34:57	O'Gara pen

SCOTLAND

15 **CHRIS PATERSON** (Edinburgh)
14 **SIMON DANIELLI** (Ulster)
13 **MAX EVANS** (Glasgow)
12 **GRAEME MORRISON** (Glasgow)
11 **THOM EVANS** (Glasgow)
10 **PHIL GODMAN** (Edinburgh)
9 **MIKE BLAIR** (Edinburgh)
1 **ALASDAIR DICKINSON** (Gloucester)
2 **ROSS FORD** (Edinburgh)
3 **EUAN MURRAY** (Northampton)
4 **JASON WHITE** (Sale, capt)
5 **JIM HAMILTON** (Leicester)
6 **ALASTAIR STROKOSCH** (Gloucester)
7 **JOHN BARCLAY** (Glasgow)
8 **SIMON TAYLOR** (Edinburgh)

IRELAND

ROB KEARNEY (Leinster) 15
TOMMY BOWE (Ospreys) 14
BRIAN O'DRISCOLL (Leinster, capt) 13
GORDON D'ARCY (Leinster) 12
LUKE FITZGERALD (Leinster) 11
RONAN O'GARA (Munster) 10
PETER STRINGER (Munster) 9
MARCUS HORAN (Munster) 1
RORY BEST (Ulster) 2
JOHN HAYES (Munster) 3
DONNCHA O'CALLAGHAN (Munster) 4
PAUL O'CONNELL (Munster) 5
STEPHEN FERRIS (Ulster) 6
DAVID WALLACE (Munster) 7
DENIS LEAMY (Munster) 8

REPLACEMENTS

Nathan Hines (Perpignan) for White (50 mins)
Chris Cusiter (Perpignan) for Blair (52 mins)
Dougie Hall (Glasgow) for Ford (57 mins)
Scott Gray (Northampton) for Barclay (67 mins)
Nick de Luca (Edinburgh) for Morrison (70 mins)

NOT USED
Murray Low (Glasgow)
Hugo Southwell (Edinburgh)

REPLACEMENTS

Jamie Heaslip (Leinster) for Leamy (31 mins)
Jerry Flannery (Munster) for Best (61 mins)
Tomás O'Leary (Munster) for Stringer (66 mins)
Geordan Murphy (Leicester) for Kearney (76 mins)

NOT USED
Paddy Wallace (Ulster)
Tom Court (Ulster)
Mick O'Driscoll (Munster)

Six Nations Championship: Round 4

	P	W	D	L	F	A	Pts
IRELAND	4	4	0	0	104	58	8
Wales	4	3	0	0	85	64	6
England	4	2	0	2	98	58	4
France	4	2	0	2	74	93	4
Scotland	4	1	0	3	67	76	2
Italy	4	0	0	4	41	120	0

ITALY **15** WALES **20**
ENGLAND **34** FRANCE **10**

Murrayfield, March 14th, 2009. Attendance :55,000
Referee Jonathan Kaplan (SA)
Touch judge Wayne Barnes (England) Carlo Damasco (Italy)
TMO Hugh Watkins (Wales)

WALES V IRELAND

MILLENNIUM STADIUM, MARCH

THE BALL ELUDES BOTH GAVIN HENSON (WALES) AND GORDON D'ARCY

IRELAND'S OSPREY TO PREY ON THE WELSH

21:03:09, MILLENNIUM STADIUM, JOHN O'SULLIVAN

TOMMY BOWE wouldn't mind being upbraided by a few of the locals when he returns to his home on the Swansea waterfront next week. To suffer those verbal slings would mean that Ireland had beaten Wales in the Six Nations Championship at the Millennium Stadium on Saturday; a victory embossed with the trappings of history, Grand Slam, Triple Crown and Championship honours.

It's not that he's been bestowed with celebrity status in the locality since moving from Ulster to the Ospreys last summer as he laughs: "I don't need to be walking around with the funny nose and the glasses. I don't think I am anywhere near the ballpark of (James) Hook and (Gavin) Henson. Mind you if we win, I could run into a few harsh comments."

Bowe is well versed with the magnitude of the task that Ireland seek to accomplish because on a weekly basis he is reminded of the talent the Welsh team that takes the field in Cardiff possesses, backboned by a host of his Ospreys' teammates. Yesterday's team announcements either side of the Irish Sea will probably appreciably increase what has been to this point a trickle of text messages. He smiles: "I'd say a bit of banter might be on its way," before explaining why this match above all others so far has a very special personal resonance.

"It's a huge game for the whole team but on an individual basis, whether this was going to be a decider or just a normal international, it was always going to be a massive match for me to come up against quite a few of my teammates. "It's something that I am looking forward to but it will be daunting enough coming up against those boys."

In Bowe's first season at the Ospreys he didn't know what to expect in relation to his new teammates when making the journey from Ulster, armed only with snippets from the newspapers. "You hear in the papers more than anything about egos and different personalities and stuff. I was a little bit worried wondering what they were all going to be like. The time I played in the Welsh match last year I hadn't talked to any of the boys, didn't know them but Lee Byrne was straight over chatting to me afterwards. He introduced himself. They're a good bunch and I'm looking forward to a bit of banter out on the pitch and hopefully a bit of fun after it. I would be friendly with a lot of the guys but more so with Jonathan Thomas, Lee Byrne, James Hook; they would be the boys I would have hung around with at various stages, going for a cup of coffee and things like that."

Bowe expects to find himself pitted against Shane Williams and knows that he's in for a difficult afternoon, although he'd be keen that the traffic wasn't all one way. "He'd be a humble guy. He's a very, very nice guy when you sit and chat to him. I was thinking I might be up against Shane which would be a nice little battle to enjoy. Shane rarely sticks on his wing so I will be seeing plenty of the boys, like Shane and Lee Byrne. Hopefully I'll get a few shots in and won't be the one taking all the punishment. They have so many dangerous players but sometimes those strengths can be a weakness as well in terms of forcing the pass.

"The amount of 50-50 passes thrown; it only takes one to come off to allow a great line break but the flip side is that one that's misplaced could lead to an error that would work in our favour. They play a great style of rugby. Obviously with Warren Gatland, they play a slightly different style (to the Ospreys). There's definitely a structure that he has put in place. Obviously I want to be involved in all the matches but it would have killed me not to be part of this game. It's the biggest game of the championship for me. Everything that accompanies this match - Grand Slam, the Championship - is huge but on a personal basis it is the one I had earmarked."

Bowe is well aware of the dangers of playing the game in his mind, like some endless loop that threatens to drain physically and emotionally. There has to be an off switch away from the training ground and video analysis duties. "No I don't like to get too caught up in it. I'll get texts from friends and family, wishing me well and telling me they'll be watching . . . asking me for tickets or what bar we'll be going to, but it is a case of switching off from that and hanging out with the boys. Within the camp it's great you don't have to be talking rugby 24/7.

The Grand Slam has been banned for the last couple of weeks because no one wants to get too ahead of themselves and it will be no different this week." Bowe will be hoping that come Saturday night, he'll be celebrating a Grand Slam, Triple Crown, Six Nations Championship, the bragging rights neatly tucked into his back pocket when he returns to Swansea.

GATLAND GRENADE NOT MEANT TO EXPLODE

21:03:09, MILLENNIUM STADIUM, **GERRY THORNLEY**

DECLAN KIDNEY could never have been a boxing promoter. The Ireland coach tends to dismiss any pre-match mind games with a shrug, a smile and a comment along the lines of, "people say things", which is in stark contrast to Warren Gatland, who can tend to become a little mischievous in match weeks, and indeed say a few things. Throwing a few grenades in the direction of England has been a particularly enjoyable pastime before Wales' last two wins over the Red Rose and viewed in that light his claim that his players disliked the Irish players more than any other can probably be interpreted as a compliment, which is what he maintained yesterday.

"I meant it as a compliment," said Gatland yesterday, though he also admitted: "I knew when I said it that it was going to get headlines. It got more of a reaction than I wanted probably. People have reacted rather than just take it with a grain of salt and a backhanded compliment." The Welsh coach cited the regularity with which the Irish provinces, especially Munster and Leinster, and the Welsh regions have bumped into each other in recent years, either in huge Heineken Cup games or in top-of-the-table Magners League games, and the way Ireland have held sway over Wales in recent years - winning seven of the last nine meetings, and five of them by over 20 points.

"The Welsh players have had some defeats by Munster and Leinster over the last few years, and also some big defeats by Ireland. They've had a few verbals and sometimes you can't say anything and you've got to take it, and wait for your opportunity. Yeah, of course they want to beat England as well. Everybody wants to beat England, but when you're playing sides on a more regular basis, that's what builds up the rivalry. It's not that they dislike them as individuals, it's just that they're a bit more passionate about wanting to beat the Irish at the moment," said Gatland.

"If you go back over history there were often times when Wales had the edge in this fixture, but what I was saying was in recognition of what the Irish provinces have achieved in recent years and what Ireland have achieved in the last decade or so. I don't see it any differently from Galwegians playing Corinthians," added Gatland, in attempting to put his comments into further context, "or the Shannon-Garryowen rivalry, where each wants to beat the other. I wasn't saying they disliked them as people, they just wanted to beat them so much. It's like when I was with Waikato, we always wanted to beat Auckland more than anybody else."

Donal Lenihan was manager to the Irish team when Gatland first became head coach in 1998, and commented yesterday: "I don't think Warren dislikes the Irish. I just thought it was vintage Warren Gatland. He likes to play mind games and have a bit of fun. It's just typical of the man. He looks to up the ante. Over the years, he has managed to stir up things before matches. You go back to the 2004 Heineken Cup semi-final at Lansdowne Road between Munster and Wasps. There were a lot of mind games going on there."

Speaking on RTÉ Radio One's Morning Ireland, Lenihan added: "It was the first time Warren had been back in Dublin since losing the Ireland job and it was quite emotional. There are times I think when he loses the run of himself. I was talking to Lawrence Dallaglio, who was his captain at Wasps, about him just a few weeks ago. Lawrence said there were times before matches when Warren came out with statements and you just said to yourself 'why did you say that' and I think this is one of those occasions. He's a very experienced coach and he knows what buttons to press," added Lenihan, who was probably on the money when adding: "On this occasion, I think it's more a case of him challenging his own players. He's trying to stir up the Welsh players. They have been on the receiving end against Irish teams in Heineken Cup and Magners League and he is trying to remind them of that. It's all mind games."

Lenihan reckoned that Kidney will quietly welcome Gatland's "grenade", adding: "I'm sure Warren has a huge amount of respect for the Irish players having worked over here for a good number of years. And I know the guys in the Irish set-up will have a lot of time for him. It's just a case of him trying to put pressure on his own Welsh players to deliver the goods.

"The likes of Brian O'Driscoll, Ronan O'Gara and Paul O'Connell have seen it and heard it all before. They have been around so long, they will only laugh at this type of thing. They will be concentrating on their own game and not letting any outside influences interfere with their preparations. A lot of the Irish players will know Gatland of old having been coached by him. They will just laugh it off. I think it will put more pressure on his own players than on the Irish team."

GORDON D'ARCY ELUDES THE WELSH COVER

'SPECTATORS RUSHED ON LIKE A SWARM OF LOCUSTS.'

20:03:09, MILLENNIUM STADIUM,

FROM THE ARCHIVES: HOW THE IRISH TIMES REPORTED THE CHAMPIONSHIP WIN OVER WALES IN 1899

AT CARDIFF on Saturday, the final game in the international championship journey was played, when Wales and Ireland were opposed for the 14th time. It is hardly necessary to refer to the other games in the tournament, but it will be recollected that Ireland and Scotland, with two wins each, were at the head of the table with Wales, boasting of a single victory, next, and England, with three losses, at the bottom of the ladder.

Thus Saturday's game, if a draw, would make Ireland champions, while if Wales should win it would make herself, Scotland, and Ireland tie for the championship honours, each with two wins and a loss. It is described below how Ireland won, as accurately as the terrible conditions obtaining would admit. By her victory Ireland wins the international championship for the third time, the years being 1895, 1896, and 1899, and the Triple Crown again comes to the Emerald Isle, this being the second time that the honour has been claimed in five years, 1894 being the initial victory.

Ireland, in consequence, equals Scotland's record, the sturdy representatives of the Thistle having also won on a couple of occasions, the years being 1891 and 1895. But the victory of the "wearers of the green" on Saturday is enhanced by a fact unique in the record of the competition. The Irish line has not been crossed during the season's games, the only point scored against us being the goal dropped off the penalty at Edinburgh by Donaldson, the Scottish captain. This speaks volumes for the defensive work of the back division, chopped and changed about as it has been, that did duty in the several matches.

A still stranger item occurs in connection with the victorious Irish team - namely, that only five players have taken part in all three games, and only one of this quintet a back. LM Magee, the captain of the team, is that back, and the two Ryans, Sealy and Byron, the forwards. There is much room for self-congratulation in the contemplation of this, and it shows beyond yea or nay that Ireland at the present time, despite the exceedingly gloomy outlook of the early part of the present season, is passing rich in first-class players all of them young and likely to be available for a number of years to come.

Possibly no match in which the Irish 15 were ever engaged excited a tithe of the interest that Saturday's game provoked. The south Welsh town presented a gay and animated appearance from an early hour on Saturday morning, and on inquiry the ready answer was to the effect that the bustle and excitement were caused by the big game which would take place in the afternoon. The weather, from a football point of view, was simply delightful, the sun, as the hour to commence approached, shining with agreeable fervour, and dissipating the cold which was rather troublesome in the early morning. The ground, too, was in excellent condition, and bore great evidence of the care expended upon it, the turf being in grand condition.

There were many thousand spectators gathered round the principal entrance when the gates were open, and in an hour there were over 20,000 spectators within the enclosure and yet an hour to pass by ere the kick-off took place. By the thousand still they came, till at 2.30 it was estimated that a further 10,000 were within the enclosures. Then an untoward event occurred, as on the popular, or river side, the palisade gave way owing to the weight of the crowd, and five or six hundred spectators rushed on like a swarm of locusts through the breach, and, to continue the simile, they as effectively destroyed everything they touched.

In a trice the reserved seats inside the palings were appropriated: next, the pressmen from all parts of the three kingdoms had to fly for their lives from fear of a terrible crush, and finally, the people in the enclosure in front of the grandstand, finding their view obstructed by the ever increasing multitude inside the palings, swarmed over the railing, demolishing the press tables, reserved chairs and every bit of woodwork that lay about.

The scene that followed "beggars all description", as the surging and impatient crowd outside the general entrance was so great that the pressure swept away turnstiles, ticket issuers, and the whole paraphernalia connected with them, and thousands of disappointed reserved seat holders rushed, ticket in hand, into the ground. Policemen and officials were swept away like matchwood before a cyclone, and at 3 o'clock when a start should have taken place, there was not as much vacant space, save on the playing pitch, as would give standing room to a child, and even the touch and goal lines were encroached upon to the extent of several feet.

Of course it would appear from all of this that the Welsh officials were to blame, but this idea would be to a great extent erroneous. A prominent member of the Welsh Union informed us on Friday night that a record crowd was expected, say between 25,000 and 30,000, but it was a physical impossibility to afford proper accommodation to the enormous crowd desiring to see the game. However, a squad of police some three or four times as large as that in use might have stemmed the tide when the breakage first took place and restored order to some degree.

It must also be said in justice to the Welsh spectators that despite the crush they behaved with every decorum, and were most dispassionate throughout. Hence the teams, having been photographed, took the ground sharp to time. The spectators were in rows 12 deep and some three feet over the touch and goal lines. This necessitated the referee, Mr Adam Turnbull (Scotland), making use of his prerogative not to start the game until the obstruction was removed. All this time a capital bass brand (Tongwynlais) were playing some pleasant selections in the centre of the ground, but the confusion all round the enclosure prevented the proper enjoyment of the music.

The trees around the ground had gradually become black with people, and even the lofty telegraph and telephone posts had their quota of enthusiastic lovers of rugby. It was ascertained at this juncture that the large party of excursionists from Dublin and the south of Ireland, who were travelling via Waterford and Milford Haven, could not arrive in time for the match, despite its late start, owing to getting befogged in the Channel. It transpired afterwards that they were just in time to see the victorious Irishmen carried shoulder high by enthusiastic expatriated countrymen to their hotel.

At 3.30 the teams, which were previously photographed, again entered the field, and, having gone round the touchlines, exhorting the people to give the necessary room, lined out as appended, and without change from the teams published on Saturday morning.

GAUGING GATLAND'S GUIDE TO IRISH WEAKNESSES

20:03:09, MILLENNIUM STADIUM, LIAM TOLAND

INDULGE ME for a moment and allow me the pleasure of drifting across the water into the Welsh camp. Let me take on the persona of the Lions' forwards coach and the current Grand Slam coach. His last nine Six Nations matches have returned eight victories, a Triple Crown, a Championship and a Grand Slam. The game he lost this year was against France in Paris, where Ireland have lost many times. This Welsh loss was by one score, five points, and against a French side bursting for a victory. Their victories, conversely, have been by 13 points over Scotland, Ireland managed it by seven; by eight over England, Ireland managed it by one.

Over the past two seasons Wales have been winning a lot of matches and have been doing it with style. Against Australia in the autumn they managed a 21-18 victory when Ireland were struggling against Argentina and being walloped by the All Blacks. This Welsh team are favourites to win tomorrow, and here's how Warren Gatland will view us.

Although the sides Ireland have met to date have not exposed our defence, having conceded a miserable three tries, it will be done tomorrow. Scotland proved by moving the point of contact left and right at speed, the Irish can look ragged. Combined with the famous Welsh ball "off the ground out of the tackle" continuity, the Irish defence will become disjointed and very tired.

Over the course of the Championship Gatland will have noticed that, after multiple phases, John Hayes and co find themselves all too often in the middle of the defensive line. Seldom have the opposition exposed this, but Gatland's side will. Let's not fool ourselves - in a match of the tightest margins Shane Williams will be searching for John Hayes just as Riki Flutey did Sébastien Chabal. It is no coincidence Flutey ended up in front of Chabal after four minutes last week on the way to England's opening try.

Expect Gatland to use Williams. It may only happen once, but in a tight game that may be enough. Jamie Heaslip's amazing try against France came when tighthead Benoit Lecouls, Chabal and Lionel Nallet were alone on their 22. The Irish centres are superb players with a spectrum of skills, but neither has a kicking game that will pressurise the Welsh. That both are world class is not the issue, but Gatland will look to expose this limitation. The "Gatland gun" defence will as always target the outside in, so a clever Irish kicking game is required to unhinge the onrushing Welsh.

The Irish kicking game will be of great interest to Gatland. His back three will adore the opportunity of fielding O'Gara's punts and then run, run, run back at them. Again, the Irish defensive system will be tested, and Gatland will have spotted peculiarities. Speaking of the Irish backline: Gatland will have noticed Ireland rely heavily on set-piece plays that require precision, incorporating a first phase (lineout) followed by ordained moves. He knows well an aggressive defence will put enormous pressure on the ball-receiver. This may force O'Gara back into the pocket. The outhalf has to remain aggressive, on the gain line and brave.

Gatland will notice, too, that the Irish rely on their front five to run at tree trunks in defence. They pursue close-in targets that evolve into slow attacking ball where the scrumhalf has to dig deep into the ruck. He will also remember how the brave Paul O'Connell picks and goes around the fringe. His big men will be waiting.

WALES CAPTAIN RYAN JONES APPEARS TO GO HIGHEST

Gatland will also have noticed the half-time scores have not flattered Ireland. France down by 10-13, Italy down by 9-14, England drawing 3-3 and Scotland ahead by only 12-9. He will realise that in the closing stretch Ireland will be at their best. Therefore, he will insist on scores on the board. Expect Stephen Jones to drop goal at will and push home every advantage by half-time.

Thank God the man in the middle is from north of the equator. Unfortunately we can't have Alain Rolland, but I'm sure Wayne Barnes will do. The Irish scrum, with the help of Jonathan Kaplan, survived against Scotland, but Barnes will have a stronger view. This will allow the 6ft 4in, 18st "one trick pony" Andy Powell to run hard at O'Gara. And, when he arrives from the bench, it will be 6ft 4in and 16st 9lb Jamie Roberts' turn to run hard. Expect Wales to use the extra five metres at the scrum. Gatland knows Munster used David Wallace out in the centre to nullify the Leinster backline in the European Cup match in 2006. And England used Joe Worsley in the same way to great effect.

So will Ireland take the same chance? Absolutely, but who'll marshal the inside channel? And more importantly, can Ireland survive without Wallace at the coalface the way Munster could? The most underrated Lion of them all, Martyn Williams, will once again prove a thorn in the Irish side. He has perfected the art of continuity, seamlessly allowing the ball to flow. If Wallace is out in the Irish backline, who will neuter Williams?

Except for a handful of times, mainly against France, the Irish back three have been very conservative, so Gatland will happily keep the ball out of touch and trust his defence (five tries conceded). Ireland's scores have been built around the lineout. Nullify it and Gatland knows Ireland will be forced into inventive play, something that hasn't been all too evident. The Irish lineout has some peculiarities to it also. Once again they have four main options, but rely heavily on O'Connell in the middle. It's worked well with speed and simplicity. But it's on the ground Gatland will notice that the Irish backrow can move up the line. Will Williams follow?

By the way, Wales have their weaknesses too, but I just happened to drift into the Welsh camp for a moment. Gatland will also realise O'Gara, O'Connell, O'Driscoll etc are an exceptional team that have all the ingredients to win. So can Ireland win? Absolutely. But will they win? Unfortunately the answer is no. Well, that's what Warren Gatland will be thinking. So what of the Welsh weaknesses? They have several, but their biggest tomorrow will be their numbers 4, 5 and 6. Ryan Jones missed the opener against Scotland, wasn't selected against the Italians and went missing against the France. He's a monster, but based on his play thus far shouldn't be starting.

May I end on this Grand Slam weekend as I've started so many weeks ago, with a little Patton: "In . . . operations, retreat is impossible; to surrender is as ignoble as it is foolish. Above all else, remember that we as attackers have the initiative, we know exactly what we are going to do, while the enemy is ignorant of our intentions and can only parry our blows. We must retain this tremendous advantage by always attacking rapidly, ruthlessly, viciously and without rest."

Once again, spare a thought for those fallen soldiers who won't be part of tomorrow's party . . .

KIDNEY JUST TOO COOL FOR GATLAND

21:03:09, MILLENNIUM STADIUM, GERRY THORNLEY

KEITH WOOD has ventured that Declan Kidney gives the impression that there's an under-14 game on today. Well, Kidney still conveyed the impression yesterday. "I'm looking forward to it alright; a free ticket," the Irish coach quipped. "It is sport, and it's what you get into it for. If Fester says that, well and good, but I do look forward to it, I enjoy watching these fellas play. I have always enjoyed watching Ireland play ever since I first saw Ireland play on a black and white tv, or maybe get to your first match. Every Saturday, when it comes around to international time, from the time you take an interest in rugby - when I was four or five - you look forward to your Five Nations or Six Nations and you get excited about matches."

Inevitably, Kidney was questioned about Warren Gatland's comments of last Tuesday, whereupon he paused and, in classic mode, said dryly: "I thought the pitch was in great order, it's a smashing stadium to play in and we're really looking forward to the game." For his part, Gatland conceded that his remarks were "probably a bit over the top."

"Perhaps I should have been a little bit tempered and said that out of all the teams in the Six Nations the team the Welsh want to beat the most is the Irish. I've nothing personal against the Irish. I've got some great friends there, my daughter was born in Ireland, so please, for the Irish, don't take it personally." Gatland wondered whether he should "take a leaf out of Declan Kidney's book". Implored not to do so by a Welsh journalist, he then added. "That's probably the way to go in the future, cliches and say nothing. That's probably, in hindsight, the way to go in terms of press conferences." It wasn't clear that this was in direct reference to Kidney, but it may be interpreted that way.

As for the match - oh yes, the match. "I think Ireland are going to try and strangle us, play set-piece rugby, O'Gara kicking, a lot of pick and go. That's the way they've been playing the game. We've got to be a little more expansive." On the eve of what is, for Ireland, a rare sighting of the Slam, Kidney maintained. "This is everybody's team," he said, "we're just lucky enough to be the ones around here. Our job is to represent everybody and let everybody's feelings go with that then."

PAUL O'CONNELL GETS READY FOR THE FRAY IN CARDIFF

TIME THE GOLDEN BOY CARRIED OFF THE GOLDEN PRIZE

21:03:09, MILLENNIUM STADIUM, GERRY THORNLEY

THERE ARE many reasons underscoring Ireland's craving for a Grand Slam today but aside from blessed relief from our general woes, the main one would be to see a tangible reward for the so-called golden generation. The players themselves probably hate that description, but approaching the 50th and last game of a decade which has seen Ireland win as many matches as the French, and more than anyone else, two players would assuredly have fitted that description any time, any era, any generation. If Ireland can't win a Grand Slam when they have Paul O'Connell and Brian O'Driscoll, you wonder if they ever will.

It's hard to believe Irish rugby has produced a better back or better forward, certainly not in the same generation. But the only way of fully satisfying their own craving for success would be a win today. That Ireland have a shot at glory today would not have been possible without a whole host of factors and individuals. But none have done more than O'Connell and O'Driscoll, who have produced four big games apiece. O'Connell has never seemed more of a force of nature than this season. His lineout work has been even more imperious than ever, likewise his ball-carrying, and it's also clear the extra work spent on handling skills with Tony McGahan at Munster has paid off. He is, as Stephen Ferris said during the week, Ireland's "go-to player". If in doubt, pass it to Paulie. If in doubt, throw it to Paulie. If in doubt, where's Paulie?

Meeting up with him earlier this week, he seemed incredibly relaxed given the week that's in it, chatting with the same honesty as you invariably get from him on the pitch. He's a credit to his family and his Munster roots. Twenty-nine years old, at the peak of his career perhaps, with 60 caps to his name and Heineken Cups with Munster, for the second of which he was captain. So you'd imagine he might not be operating under the same, seemingly almost demonic desire for success. He denies it, but he clearly is. "I'd definitely rather be younger and have a lot more time left in it, because I'm enjoying it more than ever, which is the most important thing. Yeah, but it isn't a bad place. People look back and say they've no regrets. I wouldn't look back and say I've no regrets. I think there's things that you just have to accept, that this is part of the process even though they were big disappointments at the time and you would have done things differently.

"But you appreciate that some of the things you've done subsequently may not have happened without those disappointments. But I'd like to think there's a lot more to come." Or, as a true disciple of Declan Kidney would put it - "you learn more from your defeats than your wins. That's what people don't realise sometimes, that no-one's career is up, up, up, up, up, up. There are ups and downs, and that's what makes people good decision-makers and good people to have on the field with you; the people who have been through all the bad times and the good times as well. That's important."

So, while he might like to be starting out on the journey and have a longer road in front of him, he also has a far sharper radar for the potholes and the bends. This, after all, is a team man honed, to some extent, by the individualistic drive he took to golf and swimming in his formative sporting years. "Oh yeah, everything you've done up until now is learning for your next game. It's as simple as that, and it's strange but I think the more you go on the more you realise how much there is to learn. When I was young, I suppose I was very forthright in my opinions. I still am probably, but I do realise there's an awful lot left to learn in terms of the psychological part of the game, the tactical part of the game, everything down from fitness, skills. It seems the older you get the more you realise there is to do."

In his book, Ronan O'Gara occasionally refers to his teammate as Psycho O'Connell. David Wallace and others talk of being on the end of the O'Connell scowl if they mess up a lineout call in training. You wonder how he feels about his mates portraying him as this slightly demonic or psychotic, ultra-driven professional? He looks down and laughs. "That's all a bit of a laugh. With us, if you get a slag and you get ratty about a slag it sticks. Maybe I did at the start, but I find it funny now." But, he says, they're all the same, it's just that he and Quinlan wear it on their sleeves, whereas "people would have the likes of Wally and Dunners down as happy-go-lucky guys; they are competitive, driven, edgy guys at training and on the pitch, but I suppose the public don't always see that."

Munster's first Heineken Cup was formed on a huge reservoir of emotion built up over previous near misses. The second win felt so different, he says, that it gave them a new level of confidence and this season they've learned how to peak for nearly each game, without having to dip into the emotional well off the back of a loss, or on a revenge mission. "For the first time with Munster this year that hasn't been there, and it's been very interesting from a sporting concept figuring all that out."

Now in his third season as Munster captain, he reflects on that first, difficult year and says: "I think I probably didn't understand the whole way that captaincy worked. I think I had to figure it out for myself and I probably used to take a lot on myself when I didn't need to. "I think the more important you think the role of captain is the harder you make the job for yourself. The more you rely on other people and realise their importance, the easier the job becomes. So the first year I definitely found the job hard. I probably didn't think about it enough in terms of what it takes to be a captain, so this year I've enjoyed it immensely, really immensely."

He's also much more comfortable assuming a leadership role with Ireland, as one of O'Driscoll's main lieutenants. "He's very measured and lets me do my kind of thing no matter what. Sometimes I lose it and I'd say Brian would look at me and think that's not the way he'd handle it. But he just lets me off and when he does need to talk his is a fresh voice, and vice versa."

As for the player, O'Connell says of O'Driscoll: "First and foremost, with so many teams their best player is often the guy you target in defence. So I think when you have a guy whose team need him on the attacking front but also then need him on the defensive front - and he does all the hard work better than anyone else on the team - that's massive for a team. "I think that's why all the old school kind of Munster guys always respected him. He never struggled to win those guys over because he wasn't just throwing the miss-passes and making the breaks. He was busting his hamstrings doing these ridiculous poaches with 20-stone guys trying to knock him off the ball. So straight away he has respect from everyone."

In contrast to the great one's meteoric rise up the international ranks, O'Connell's was more of a slow burner, but looking back, he still can't believe how lucky he was, how so many things fell into place at the right time. He'd played under-10s to 12s with Young Munster, concentrating on golf and swimming until resuming rugby with Ardscoil Rís at 16. And if I hadn't gone back at 16, it would have been very hard to go back at 18 or 19, and I was very lucky to get into Irish Schools and once your name is in the hat there coaching at Irish schools level is class."

On the back of that came the Munster under-21s and the Ireland under-21s. The way he describes it, it's a bit like a production line, once you hop aboard the only way is up. He sat on the bench for Young Munster for a year after school, and cut his teeth in the Munster Junior Cup, which Munsters won, and had three pretty full seasons with his club, "important times" on his learning curve, coming up against old school coaches and players, while still reaping the trappings of the academy. The makings of him in many ways. The AIB League has to be a cornerstone for people coming through," he says with utter conviction. "It was for me. Things like going up playing Ballymena away. Playing against Mary's, with Mal (O'Kelly) and Trevor Brennan, was phenomenal for me at 19 or 20."

He came into the League at the right time too, when the Munster forwards were all returning to the club game with new ideas, new lifting techniques or whatever, and O'Connell was playing with or against them six or seven times a season. "I didn't go in like (Anthony) Foley did at 18, into an absolute bloodbath of a tournament."

Even when breaking into the Munster pack he found himself surrounded by seven internationals all the while, in time honoured fashion, biding his time. "We were chatting about this last Sunday over dinner, and we were talking about what a big jump it is for the academy guys, and it's only the guys with real, massive mental strength that really rate themselves."

He cites Donncha Ryan, Keith Earls, Tomás O'Leary. "Like, you've got to be so confident in your ability and so mentally strong to make that jump, whereas for me there were so many little stepping stones." Some days that formed him, stand out. Of his Munster debut, a friendly against Bath, he says, "I had an absolute shocker" and recalls a restart slipping through his hands, bouncing off his knee and travelling forward 20 yards. His competitive debut, as a late sub in the first Celtic League game of the 2001-2002 season away to Edinburgh, he remembers more fondly.

"I stole a lineout, with five minutes to go, made a carry, kind of stepstepped a guy and made about eight or nine metres. I think we won a penalty off it or something and I remember Quinny patting me on the back. I think Quinny said something about me in the huddle as we were waiting for Rog to kick the penalty. That for me . . . I remember going in and getting my phone out of my bag before I changed to ring home, because it wouldn't have been televised or anything. Gaillimh, Claw, Frankie, Wally, Quinny were all playing. Dunners had just come on five minutes before me. I don't even remember the name of the ground."

His try-scoring debut for Ireland would follow in February 2002 at home to today's opponents, but days like that were as much the making of him as the 2003 Grand Slam shootout against England. He still recalls coming on with the score 18-6 and it finishing 42-6. Ireland are, he says, "much different" from what they were that day. "I don't even remember what I would have been thinking back then. Niallo was probably hoping I'd make an impact and maybe I was just happy to be coming on." Somehow you doubt it.

"I suppose we've grown up. It is a big game at the weekend but it's just a game still. When you're young you say in interviews 'we'll just take each game as it comes' without probably appreciating how important it is, but I think probably we've been doing that." So much of what they do now is player-driven, whereas then,

A YOUNG IRISH SUPPORTER CELEBRATES HIS TEAM'S SUCCESS

he says, the older guys had to be cajoled into it. And as for 61 years. "There's just been so many big games now, you know what you have to do and we'll go out and do it, and hopefully we'll come out the right side of it.

"I don't even know how to explain it, in terms of why we aren't overawed. Some guys maybe are back in their rooms but there's just been so many big games and maybe in the past teams didn't have as many big games behind them. You need to seize momentum. Their game is about momentum and pressure, and we can't let that build on us. Very often pressure makes you produce big games. I don't think it's something that should make anybody freeze, I think it's a great situation to be in because everybody will be looking to bring absolutely everything they have to the game.

"Y'know, family, the motivation of playing with friends, winning with friends, the fact we haven't done it in so long, you bring everything you have to the table on these big days and then hopefully because of that you produce a big performance." Seize momentum and seize the moment. No better man.

EIGHTY MINUTES TO IMMORTALITY

21:03:09, MILLENNIUM STADIUM, GERRY THORNLEY

ENOUGH TALKING. Now, at last, the game of truth. It's been a long time coming this week so, particularly after all the brouhaha, this evening's little title showdown in Cardiff can't come quickly enough. This may simply be the biggest game of these Ireland players' lives, particularly if they win. The expectations are at fever pitch and everything is set fair. Cardiff is awash in sunshine, with temperatures soaring to unseasonably high teens. It could almost have been Rome yesterday - well, maybe not - as the advance party of a 15-20,000 Green Army invasion landed.

Opportunity knocks for Ireland to remove that 61-year-old monkey, and given there have been only four chances to emulate the heroes of 1948, it's not stretching things to say that, for Irish rugby, such possibilities only come along once in a lifetime. At any rate, this is a career-defining game. It's that big. The case for including Brian O'Driscoll, Paul O'Connell, et al, atop the pantheon of Irish rugby greats would be conclusive.

Granted, opportunity knocked in 2003 when Ireland met England in a last day, winner-takes-all. But this is a stronger all round side than that Ireland team, and mentally this cannot be viewed as nearly as daunting a task as facing the World Cup champions-in-waiting back in '03. Wales are good, but they're not that good, not just yet anyway. Furthermore, Munster have stormed the Millennium Stadium twice to win Heineken Cups and the playing staff and coaching ticket are heavily populated with people who have vast experience of games such as this. All the brickbats from hereabouts might well backfire. They can handle the pressure.

Nonetheless, as in '03, the toughest part has been kept to last, and the downside of this is that Ireland could win the championship in defeat, were Wales to win by 13 points or less. That would be a huge anticlimax, for although they won't publicly countenance such an outcome, one imagines in their minds it would serve as a disappointment. A first championship in 24 years would be duly recognised as a fine achievement, but having given themselves this shot at immortality, it's almost a win or bust scenario.

One can also readily make a strong case as to why Wales might win. Warren Gatland has stopped the selectorial whims and simply plumped for his best team. His Grand Slam team. All bar one started the win in Croke Park last year. The Gavin Henson-Tom Shanklin midfield partnership, for example, have won all 12 of their Tests together.

The conditions are exactly as they would want them and they clearly intend having an almighty go: quick lineout ball, quick taps, kicking to keep the ball in play, a scorching high tempo using the full width of the pitch and targeting Ronan O'Gara, as Wasps did to Munster in the 2004 Heineken Cup semi-finals and as Wales did last year in Croke Park. One imagines David Wallace will be filling that channel.

The Welsh attack game looks more developed than Ireland's, which has not repeated the opening feats against France in their last two outings. Shane Williams and Lee Byrne, sure to be hitting the line like no other fullback has done to Ireland thus far, have to be closed down quickly. Wales' sharper pace out wide is also manifest in their more ambitious counterattacking game, and recalling how the kick-and-chase gave Scotland opportunities, the kicking game by O'Gara, Tomás O'Leary and Rob Kearney has to be either very long or, more likely, short enough to chase hard.

First and foremost, perhaps, Ireland have not started any of their last three games well, and were Wales to score a try early on, build up an initial lead, then much of their old swagger will return. It wouldn't be much fun playing any kind of catch-up against their defence. If not, though, Wales could become frustrated, for they have gradually lost some of their autumn momentum, especially over the last two matches. So impressive has Ireland's conditioning and stamina been that they look the match of Wales physically and, mentally, perhaps look stronger.

In that, Stephen Ferris has been a barometer, yet they are becoming uncannily like a Munster team in their capacity to absorb pressure and then make their turn count. The collisions will be king. They usually are, but all the more so when Wales play, for like all of the Warren Gatland/Shaun Edwards teams, their game is based on generating go-forward momentum through them.

But England, to a large degree, France hugely so, and even the Italians showed how the Welsh can be strangled, and, by taking a decisive hold on the game through strong set-pieces, with O'Connell, Wallace and co patiently working their way through the phases, be it pick and go, one-off runners or launching the freaks in midfield, O'Driscoll and Gordon D'Arcy, Ireland have been the best stranglers in the competition. Reacting to referee Wayne Barnes, who is more severe on players going off their feet, will be critical.

Ireland may also need more of a mix, and to score a couple of tries, but there has been little evidence recently that their attack can help them over this last hurdle. But they have scored two more than Wales and do have tries in them. You sense they have what it takes to get there. Men on a mission.

RONAN O'GARA, STRIKES AN ANGELIC POSE AFTER HIS MATCH WINNING DROP GOAL

IRELAND DELIVER ON A GRAND SCALE

23:03:09, MILLENNIUM STADIUM, GERRY THORNLEY

IRELAND. GRAND Slam champions. Sounds nice, yes? The barbs can be put to one side now and Irish rugby can hold its head higher than ever before. No more references to Ireland being chokers, and there'll never be a mention of 62 years. The golden generation have delivered its greatest day.

First off, this success was about the team. The squad. They're all stars really, but there are no egos. The team adds up to more than the sum of its considerable parts. Modesty forbids of course, for Declan Kidney would detest almost any praise being heaped on him. But basking in the glow of a great day for everyone, and one of his mantras is that this is for everybody, he was asked what was the ingredient that pulled Ireland through the tautest of three one-score wins in a row. You could have guessed the first word out of his mouth. "Honesty, trust, hard work, willingness to go the extra little bit. It's like I said earlier, nobody was blaming anybody. We had none of that, no cliques, no nothing. We gave it a go in the best way possible. You cannot overestimate honesty."

Brian O'Driscoll spoke of Kidney knowing his strengths and delegating, but also admitted he had "an X factor". However he helps achieve this honesty amongst the group, be it as a facilitator, organiser, manager or coach, his teams usually have it in spades. That's some trick. Honesty of effort, an unwavering refusal to let down a teammate, being able to look each other in the eye and belief in each other. These traits have transcended all five wins of the Grand Slam odyssey.

Critical to that was a squad get-together in Enfield before Christmas. Kidney explained: "That was our opportunity," he admitted. "When November was over, we sat down. I have a brilliant bunch of team leaders, Brian, Rog, Paul, Rory. We sat down with Paul (McNaughton) and we had a good, frank discussion. We opened it up, asked the players what they think: 'Let's put it out on the table, lads'. It was nothing hugely scientific. I'm not saying I'm a management consultant or anything, but it was just saying 'Let's be honest with one another now. What are the (wrong) things?' You'd be surprised that by talking about it, and a little bit of slagging, all of a sudden a whole lot of doors were opened, and we just have some craic now."

Having ended a seemingly interminable 61-year hiatus peculiar to Irish rugby, Kidney talked about feeding into what it is to wear an Irish jersey, and the honour, sweat and toil that goes into it. "I'd be a believer that you don't ever own a jersey, you don't ever nail down a jersey. You have it for one afternoon, and that's your chance. You leave your DNA in it, and what way do you leave it? Hopefully the lads today have added their little bit to it, so whoever fills it in our next match in May, they'll feel that onus on them to represent it."

Kidney was so humble and proud at the same time, and so inclusive, he even mentioned the groundwork done by his predecessor Eddie O'Sullivan as well as the mini-rugby coaches who first gave these players their love of rugby. Some people want power for themselves, some want it to make a difference. In a country seemingly short of true leaders in recent times, Kidney is a class act. Just what the country needs really.

In many ways Ireland's overdue Grand Slam merely highlighted better than any of the near misses how difficult they are to achieve. O'Driscoll repeatedly talks of the fine lines between winning and losing, the small moments that can decide a game, and this team, this squad, are all about the inches and the small moments. Ronan O'Gara had reminded the players that morning that these chances don't come along very often, especially for the older players. They couldn't regret not giving everything, they would be pushed beyond the pain barrier.

You think of Tommy Bowe and Brian O'Driscoll tackling Simon Danielli and Phil Godman in Murrayfield, and on Saturday of Luke Fitzgerald bravely putting his body in front of Mike Phillips in the 75th minute, thereby halting his momentum, and of Peter Stringer making the recovery tackle to prevent the Welsh scrumhalf scoring a try which might have put Wales 19-14 in front with less than five minutes to go. Their honesty, along with O'Connell and Wallace punching the ball up, and Marcus Horan, Jerry Flannery, John Hayes, Donncha O'Callaghan, Denis Leamy and Jamie Heaslip working their socks off to recycle the ball, made it possible for O'Gara to land the match-winning drop goal.

"I'd an awful lot of time to think about it," O'Gara recalled afterwards. "I was roaring for the ball for 30, 40, 50 seconds, I don't know how long, from 15 metres in. But then Strings showed great composure, I think he knew what he was looking to do. I took about 15 yards from Strings, they obviously got a running start. No way that ref was going to give a penalty; they were well offside. So I had to concentrate on getting the ball up rather than driving through like a normal drop kick."

So much for cracking under pressure then, as the Welsh barbs had been suggesting. "Crack under pressure? I've won two European Cup finals under pressure, not one of these Welsh fellas have played in a European Cup final. What are they basing this on? They've won Grand Slams maybe. They talked the talk this week but they didn't walk the walk. I'm particularly happy in that regard."

There was still, of course, the drama of Stephen Jones' penalty attempt with the last kick of the game, and O'Gara's sympathy and embrace of Jones gave the lie to the notion that they dislike each other. Not even going to the theatre or the movies can throw up drama on this scale. Only great sporting occasions can do so, and everything about Saturday's finale belongs in the pantheon of great Irish sporting moments. We thought Munster reaching their Holy Grail wouldn't be bettered but it has been.

The sport that unites Catholic, Protestant and dissenter has had its day of days. Pity anybody who can't enjoy it. Some day.

TENSION TO THE LAST DROP AS IRELAND DELIVER

23:03:09, MILLENNIUM STADIUM,

GERRY THORNLEY

WALES 15 IRELAND 17

THEY COULDN'T do it nice and easily, could they? In America, they would be known as a cardiac team, who seem to thrive in taut thrillers, taking themselves and the rest of us through the emotional wringer right up until the last minute. If the truth be told, watching Ireland should come with a Government health warning. But even by the standards of these 'Drama Kings,' the final leg in the Grand Slam odyssey of 2009 beggared belief. Talk about a climax. John Grisham couldn't have scripted it, or if he had done so in advance he'd have been laughed out of it.

Ireland, of course, had been here before in what was a near identikit repeat of the 2003 endgame between Stephen Jones and Ronan O'Gara. When Jones' drop goal put Wales ahead with four minutes and 40 seconds left, the one consolation was Ireland had enough time to save the dream. More than anything, you knew they had a bottomless well of self-belief, rugby savvy and physical and mental strength to do so. Somehow, the cardiac team would patiently work O'Gara into field goal range.

Ironically, given Wales reject kicks to touch as a badge of honour, Jones conceded a lineout on their own 22 when he sliced his kick out on the full. The next part you could have scripted. Paul O'Connell plucked another throw out of the air, the pack rumbled, O'Gara went into the pocket and Peter Stringer pulled the strings as he does. First the scrumhalf located David Wallace closer to the Welsh sticks - and no better man than Wallace to set up the last ruck - then what followed was almost pre-ordained. It was a sweetly struck drop goal by O'Gara - no better man again - which made light of the 61-year-old hoodoo and the massive responsibility on the outhalf's shoulders, all the more so as he had been targeted, roughed up and sledged for much of the previous 80 minutes to come through with some sumptuous kicks out of hand and then that. What cojones.

What followed was the scary part. There seemed little chance of Wales penetrating the green line or working Jones back into drop goal range, whereupon Wayne Barnes penalised Paddy Wallace for fringing. While that decision, as with most of the penalties against Ireland, was correct, like many of the Englishman's calls, he seemed to be more intent on refereeing the team in green than the one in red. That made the penalty count 15-5, and 8-1 in the second period. Ireland, despite playing more of the rugby and especially so in opposition territory, were afforded only one kick at goal by Mr Barnes in the entire 80 minutes, whereas Wales had six penalty shots. Go figure.

Nothing encapsulated his apparent lack of even-handedness more than the rash of penalties which brought Wales back into the game after Ireland's 14-point double whammy inside two minutes had turned a 6-0 half-time deficit into a 14-6 lead. First, there was the reversed penalty against Donncha O'Callaghan, for pushing Mike Phillips after the whistle, one of about 30 such incidents on a tetchy afternoon which rather suggested these two sides are not especially fond of each other. Welsh flanker Dafydd Jones was involved in most of them,

IRISH SUPPORTERS ACCLAIM THEIR HEROES IN CARDIFF

yet Barnes spoke to him once. It was a highly selective piece of refereeing, and one which left a bemused O'Connell shaking his head in disbelief.

The next three-pointer was against Jamie Heaslip for taking out a lifter but his eyes were clearly on the ball in stepping backwards, whereupon he was shunted from behind by Ian Gough. But the last one might have obliged Paddy Wallace to emigrate. Five metres inside halfway, it looked well within Gavin Henson's range, but he had missed from nearer the touchline earlier and Stephen Jones was perhaps too keen to atone for his kick out on the full. Slight relief at seeing Jones address the ball turned to an explosion of joy when his kick began to die just short of the posts. A nation could breathe again.

Overall, Ireland deserved it. They won more ball, had more territory, took six of the Welsh throws, played the better rugby and, in a high octane collision of two mighty defences, managed to score the game's two tries. Once again, for the fifth game running, the team's twin totems, Brian O'Driscoll and Paul O'Connell delivered in spades. Given his form, Stephen Ferris would have been a loss to any team, except for having an inspired Denis Leamy to replace him. Leamy appeared to be everywhere, involved in so many big plays, and was instrumental in Ireland winning the game on the deck.

The honesty and work ethic of the Munster foot soldiers was immense, none more so than the remarkable John Hayes, and Gordon D'Arcy was his old self again. Ireland went into the back yard of the reigning Grand Slam champions and imposed themselves early on, but having seen O'Gara miss a penalty and O'Driscoll's try-scoring offload to Luke Fitzgerald deemed forward, turned around trailing to two Stephen Jones penalties.

Until last week, Ireland hadn't won after trailing at half-time for nine years, but as we know, they are also a secondhalf team, and especially a third quarter team, which is in part credit to their coaching staff. Relentless pack pressure and close-in rumbling culminated in O'Driscoll burrowing over for another close range try: credit to Barnes here, for he was the only one in the ground that saw it might have been a try. Ireland's clever targeting of Shane Williams' wing in the air, all the more so after Lee Byrne's costly departure, saw his fellow Osprey Tommy Bowe make a stunning catch on the run from O'Gara's deft kick - in terms of skill, the high point of the match.

Cue Barnes' concerto and the gradual disintegration of the lead, O'Gara's coup de grace and the last kick drama. Never in doubt.

TEARS OF JOY GREET HEROIC PERFORMANCE

23:03:09, MILLENNIUM STADIUM, **LIAM TOLAND**

"I'M IN tears. Really I am bawling crying here. . ." said my brother Niall in the Millennium Stadium, Cardiff. The fact he had no ticket when departing Ireland and managed to gain access to both the stadium and the pre-match BBC buildup in Cardiff's clubhouse didn't surprise me; the fact he was crying did! He wasn't the only one. Mark, a mate from Belfast, texted me: "First time I have cried after a game of rugby. Wonderful . . . EXHAUSTING!"

Sport is cruel and it was never more so on Saturday as the pendulum for disaster swung towards Wales and then Ireland. Remember the bouncing ball that went Tommy Bowe's way against Scotland that stifled Chris Paterson's certain run to the line. Well, it bounced again, this time the result of video analysis (Maith an buachaill Mervyn Murphy) and Ronan O'Gara's precision. But when it bounced Bowe was once again at its pitch. What a score and what timing.

This was truly an all-Ireland victory where players drawn from throughout the island were instrumental in victory. It's no coincidence that the three critical scores were contributed by a Leinster man, an Ulster man and finally a Munster man. That Tommy Bowe straddles the border in Monaghan, is a darling of Ulster and plies his trade in the Ospreys makes for wonderful symmetry. Not to mention the Belfast born President of Ireland Mary McAleese handing over the trophy flanked by Prince William of Wales. Sixty-one years of waiting has changed a lot in our little island.

Is it important to figure out why Ireland won? Probably not. Did they deserve to? Absolutely. But did Wales deserve to lose? Hardly. In GAA parlance a draw would have been the fairest result. But then the old GAA dictum comes to mind "you have to lose one before you win one." Well this Ireland team have lost their fair share and all those experiences helped bring them out on top yesterday. Wales were six points up at half-time, despite Ireland's field position and were looking threatening. It's hard to know what effect Andy Powell's absence may have had, but, as expected, O'Gara's channel was targeted.

The Irish stepped up for each other, covered each other, all seeming to know each other's weakness and all happy to shoulder the responsibility. Some months back an error from an Irish player drew derision. But now immediate cover up was instinctive, 'Brothers in Arms'. If Powell's absence was important Lee Byrne's departure was key. Something about Gavin Henson gives me the willies and to have him as the last line of defence is very, very unnerving. As the game ebbed and flowed I once again drifted to the 'speech of inches'. Both sets of players battled for every square inch available on the pitch.

Both teams laid out their different styles very early. Before the game I felt that Ireland's four, five and six were the key differences between winning and losing. But that would be far too simplistic in a game that swung in everyone's favour. The Welsh second rows, Ian Gough and Alun Wyn Jones, were physically immense where their tackle count was both high and ferocious. Gough's fourth minute hit on Jerry Flannery was a serious statement of intent. But their lineout!

Wales had 22 lineouts to Ireland's 10. Similar to corner kicks in soccer this is an indicator of strength. Wales's enormous penalty advantage of 15-5 gave them the platform of attacking lineouts. One wonders what might have transpired if John Hayes, Paul O'Connell, Donncha O'Callaghan and co hadn't stolen six Welsh lineouts and messed up the remainder of them. As each time Wales spurned a chance to get their game going my mind drifted to Warren Gatland. What the hell was he doing all week when his lineout required such major surgery? Hot air Warren! Remember he's a hooker with 140 appearances for Waikato and 17 for the All Blacks. Did the failing Welsh lineout cost them the match? Well no other aspect of their game was so prone to Irish influence. A little more focus in South Africa I hope.

Ironically it was their appalling lineout that provided all but one of their scores. With the exception of Stephen Jones's drop goal, the Welsh points arrived from penalties at the lineout. Bizarrely these penalties were awarded on the shambolic Welsh put in. But credit must go to all, first to the Irish who bounced back after half-time to steal the march and then to the Welsh who clawed their way back. And finally to both outhalves, Stephen Jones and Ronan O'Gara.

I recall the Chicago Bulls and their six-time winning NBA championships. On three of those finals with seconds remaining on the clock and with the world watching and waiting it was Michael Jordan who stepped forward. He did so with the opposition clearly expecting it but they couldn't prevent it. At six foot and 13 stone, O'Gara is no Michael Jordan, but, with all the pressure on his shoulders he delivered, braver than ever.

Once again the breakdown has provided an enthralling sideshow. And once again the man in the middle has provided a very different opinion. Both sides were allowed to drift offside, but particularly on the fringes. Countless times defending players inched their way unfettered past Wayne Barnes. As the pace and intensity

IRELAND COACH DECLAN KIDNEY SHARES A JOKE WITH DONNCHA O'CALLAGHAN

of the international game increases the laws must be kept as simple as possible. I hope the IRB address the obvious imbalance between referees.

Finally, as a 13-year-old I recall the passion and pride of the 1985 Triple Crown winning team. I remember the lineout from Ciaran Fitzgerald to Brian Spillane and subsequent run by Donal Lenihan deep into English territory. I remember the famous drop goal from Cork man Michael Kiernan to clinch the title. But I also remember the 1987 RWC where, to a 15-year-old, winning the cup was the obvious next step.

But it wasn't to be. They were tough times in the 80s, much like now. My great hope is that we can kick on. Our lineout is outstanding, our defence likewise but we need our scrum to survive obvious retirements and, of course, there's the ever evolving need for 'continuity, counterattack and competition for places'. It's great to be Irish.

A DROP OF MAGIC LEADS TO 59 SECONDS OF MADNESS

23:03:09, MILLENNIUM STADIUM, **MARY HANNIGAN**

TRACY PIGGOTT'S pre-match chat with Mick Galwey in Cardiff on Saturday now seems like, ooh, 61 years ago, and that's roughly by how many years viewers would have aged when the man they call Gaillimh responded to a request for a prediction. "Ah," he smiled, "a last minute drop goal from Ronan O'Gara will do us." The MERE notion of that eventuality, well, eventuating quite probably put the nation's collective heart crossways in its mouth, the prospect of the agony extending that deep in to the evening inconceivably, horrifically gruesome.

By all means, dropkick us Ronan through the goalposts of life, but do it a bit earlier than the last 60 seconds. Preferably with heaps of time left - like, say, two minutes.

Two minutes to go.

Ryle Nugent: "Horan . . . Wallace . . . Ireland in position . . . this MUST be it . . . this MUST be it for Ronan O'Gara . . . drop . . . at . . . goal . . . Grand Slam . . . at . . . stake . . . HE'S GOOOOOOT IIIIIIIIIT!!!!!!!!"

"YEEEeeeeEEEESSssssSSSS!!!!!!!!!!," said Tony Ward, leaving us wondering which side he was supporting.

"WHOOOooooOOO HOOOooooOO!!!!!," said Ryle, ensuring he'd never again receive a welcome in the valleys.

"OOOOOOOOOH!!!," said Tony, so high pitched it sounded like he'd actually popped.

"WOULD. YOU. BELIEEeeeeEEEVE. THAT," asked Ryle.

Us: "NOOOOOOOooooooo!" ("But we've still got two minutes to go," whispered Tony, so hushed it sounded like he'd just fainted). By our calculations two minutes = 120 seconds, which, in the scheme of things, isn't all that much, except when it's 120 seconds of excruciating, unendurable, insufferable hell.

Sixty seconds later.

"No penalties," pleaded Tony, his voice going all tremolo.

"No penalties now," screamed Ryle, his voice long since gone tremolo.

One second later.

Ryle: "Penalty to Wales."

The camera picked out Jack Kyle in the crowd, shaking his head like a dog after a swim. We thought of one of Jack's 1948 teammates, Paddy Reid, who had reminisced about that Grand Slam-winning campaign earlier in the day with Keith Wood over on the BBC. He recalled the game in Twickenham, Ireland were leading 11-5, "we had them beaten," he said. Then Dicky Guest intercepted an Irish pass, ran almost the length of the field to score, it was converted, Ireland's lead reduced to a point. "We nearly wet our pants," said Paddy.

Sixty-one years on and, well, we understood the discomfort that Paddy and his pals had endured. "Wales have a penalty to win the Triple Crown and break Irish hearts," said Ryle, so dolefully the nation contemplated flushing itself down the loo. "Aw. I. Don't. Believe. It," said Tony, the Victor Meldrew of the RTÉ commentary team.

Not that we were clock-watching, but the penalty was awarded with the time at 79:11; Stephen Jones struck the ball at 80:07; it neared the posts at 80:10. That was almost a whole minute. And during that eternity the birds on the trees stopped tweeting and the nation's heart, by now firmly slotted crossways in its mouth, stopped beating.

Da dum, da dum, da dum, da dum, da dum . . .

Yow know that film The Day the Earth Stood Still? Exactly.

"This will be the final act," said Ryle, "it's come down to this. All the dreams and all the hopes and all the aspirations of this Irish Grand Slam effort on Stephen Jones making or not making this kick."

"Be prepared to have your nerve endings put through a blender," Ryle had warned us before the game, but little did he and we know then that having our nerve endings put through a blender would have been quite a pleasurable experience compared to this. But all the while, through that lifetime that was those 59 seconds, you knew, come what may, you'd remember it forever, good or bad.

And as the kick approached the posts you fixed your eyes on the touch judges' flags because, by now, you couldn't tell what planet you lived on, never mind whether Jones' effort had gone over. They crouched, they studied, they exchanged a quick glance, and perhaps prompted by Tony's strangled cry of "yeeeeEEEEEeeeessssSSSSsssssss" they kept their flags lowered, and you exhaled so violently a hurricane would have seemed like a breeze. Magical.

"Sixty-one years awaiting, how sweet this moment is," said Ryle, as the nation reached for its oxygen mask.

"Don't come back with your cameras because we're lying on the floor," pleaded Tom McGurk, "Brent Pope is having cardiac arrest at the moment."

"We're nearly in tears, it means that much," said Brent. "Aw, I thought I was going to have another Seamus Darby moment, deprived right at the death," laughed Conor O'Shea, the Kerry in him still haunted by that last minute Offaly goal in the 1982 All Ireland final. (As Lloyd Bentsen might have put it, "Stephen Jones, I served with Seamus Darby: I knew Seamus Darby; Seamus Darby was a friend of mine. Stephen Jones, you're no Seamus Darby.") George Hook, meanwhile, was stretched. Declan Kidney wasn't. "If you have honesty and hard work, God knows what will turn your way," he told Tracy, his serenity making us wonder if he'd been off powdering his nose for those last couple of minutes.

It left George concluding that "if Kidney had gone for the priesthood instead of teaching, he'd be Pope". Not Brent, His Holiness. And come to think of it, yes, 'His Holiness' will do nicely. But next time, our beloved Holiness, tell your outhalf to dropkick us through the goalposts of life a bit earlier. Aside from that complaint, thanks for the majestic memories.

NOT A HINT OF BEGRUDGERY AS MEDIA EXALT TEAM'S GRAND VIRTUES

23:03:09, MILLENNIUM STADIUM, **PHILIP REID**

IT'S NICE to be liked and, after a spell as the outcasts of Europe and the butt of jokes in the City about our economic outlook, Ireland - or, more pertinently, the Irish rugby team - managed to lift the doom and gloom as newspapers in Britain and France extolled the Grand Slam-winning team's virtues with not a hint of begrudgery to be found anywhere. Just like old times, really. If there was the sense generally that Ireland were due a Grand Slam, there was also the acceptance that they had earned it through their own deeds.

Under the headline, "Intestinal fortitude allows Kidney's men to finally expel chokers' tag," Paul Hayward in the Observer wrote: "Strictly, a Grand Slam is a mere adornment to a championship title. Ireland had won four of those since the post-war side of Jack Kyle and co swept the board in the old Five Nations tournament. "There is, though, a special magic to a perfect 5-0 record, especially to a country smeared by sport's most unwanted tag: that of chokers." He continued: "That insult has been removed, if it was ever right in the first place. At no point in this scintillating game did Ireland lack intestinal fortitude . . . . this was an Irish performance of immense courage and resolve."

In the French sports daily L'Equipe, Bertrand Lagacherie wrote that Ireland "gave a lesson of courage and selflessness" and made the point that Ireland's win was "the revenge of a (golden) generation that had previously missed all its major appointments." Lagacherie wrote, "this gifted generation, led by the gang of 'O' - the O'Driscoll, O'Connell, O'Gara and others - was to lead Irish rugby to the highest level" and made the point that Declan Kidney's appointment as manager gave "hope to players who seemed not to believe in their collective capabilities".

In the Sunday Telegraph, Paul Ackford wrote of a "wonderful, wonderful match with a climax as good as any in Six Nations history. The upshot of it all is that Ireland are Grand Slam champions, 61 years of longing ended with a performance of courage and composure. Ronan O'Gara scored the winning points with a drop goal, but this was a magnificent team effort." Ackford added: "If anyone still has doubts about the courage of the modern rugby player and the gladiatorial nature of the big games, the first quarter would have dispelled those reservations. The start was fantastically confrontational."

Patrick Collins, in the Mail on Sunday, was similarly impressed by the manner of Ireland's long-awaited Grand Slam win. He wrote, "on a Cardiff evening of relentless tension and improbable drama, Ireland delivered their glorious Slam. And the prize which had eluded them for 61 years finally yielded to the force of their will and the scope of their talents".

Collins called it "a fierce, compelling and frequently brutal contest" which "withheld its result until the final seconds of the final minute", adding: "A team led by Brian O'Driscoll and bullied into glory by the astonishing Paul O'Connell had passed its final test . . . . these fine players, along with the likes of Stephen Ferris and Jerry Flannery, Luke Fitzgerald, Tommy Bowe and the rest, could take their place alongside the heroes of old. Where

RONAN O'GARA AND BRIAN O'DRISCOLL HOLD THE SIX NATIONS TROPHY ALOFT

the great characters of Irish rugby, from Willie Duggan and Moss Keane to Tony Ward and Ollie Campbell, had repeatedly tried and frustratingly failed, the victors of 2009 would be forever bracketed with the men of '48."

And James Corrigan in the Independent on Sunday reckoned that the Grand Slam achievement "was one of the island's proudest sporting occasions; if not its very proudest". Andrew Baldock in Scotland on Sunday wrote that "a new chapter in Ireland's rugby history had been written in blood and sweat and finally in tears of ecstasy. This is what sport is all about. You might get better rugby matches than Ireland's 17-15 victory over Wales. But rarely do they come laced with more thrills, more edge-of-the-seat tension and more drama than we witnessed as a Six Nations of mediocrity served up a finale to remember".

WE ARE A GREAT TEAM NOW. THERE IS SO MUCH TO BE SAID FOR A CLOSE TIGHT UNIT

23:03:09, MILLENNIUM STADIUM, **JOHN O'SULLIVAN**

ROB KEARNEY, Tommy Bowe and Denis Leamy are scattered to the four corners of the mixed zone in the bowels of the Millennium Stadium surrounded by a phalanx of tape recorders, each player holding individual court to sundry media. Although they are unaware of what each other is saying there is a familiar theme that peppers their conversation as they independently refer to a special bond, fostered by coach Declan Kidney and his management team but eagerly embraced by the players. It is the glue that allowed a group of Ireland players to win a Grand Slam in Cardiff.

The genesis for Saturday's triumph was a meeting at a hotel in Enfield last December that incorporated a full and frank exchange of views. Kearney takes up the story. "It was massive. We were there for three days and we did 45 minutes on the pitch. That's really where a lot of the groundwork was done. That was one of the occasions which went a long way to building a team. A lot of people were laying things down the line, just being truthful and honest. I think honesty is the bottom line in a lot of these things. There were a lot of things thrown from both ends but it's the sign of a great team that you can take those things on board and learn from them."

Ireland's fullback singled out the outstanding work by the backroom team, coaches, medical staff and analysts that facilitated the team's development and charted an unbeaten journey through the Six Nations. He also sought to explain the input and impact that Kidney has enjoyed since taking over the reins. "I just think we're a great team now. There's so much to be said for a close, tight unit. When the chips are down that's when you need to be playing with your friends. Over the last six months since he's come in, I can certainly say that everyone I play with now is a friend rather than a colleague."

Kearney also highlighted the input of Ronan O'Gara both before and during the match. "He said that on Wednesday or Thursday that you would be sitting on your couch at home and only then would you realise potentially what we could have done for our country. It was simple but effective." And what of the winning drop goal? "I don't think it was ever in doubt. I felt he did really well today. Even though they did target him, he stood up to it and he'll be remembered for that drop goal for life."

Leamy also addresses O'Gara's seminal intervention: "When there is five minutes left on the clock, the game isn't over. There was every chance that we could get possession and create a chance for ourselves. We did that, got the position and Rog, well there's no better man to have in the right place. He chipped it over a wall of defenders . . . great moment.

"I was in a ruck and just got up in time to watch and block some fella on the blindside. I was fairly knackered at that stage. From where I was standing, I looked at the wall of defenders and didn't think he was going to get it. He chipped it beautifully; bit of a sand wedge, brilliant. It is probably the one memory I will take away from the day, Rog's drop goal. It's a magic moment in Irish sport and we will be seeing that once or twice again."

For Leamy it was a marvellous end to a week of uncertainty, only being given medical clearance to play on the Friday from the shoulder injury he sustained against Scotland. "I wasn't expecting to come on after eight minutes but Stephen Ferris got a bad injury. It's very hard to describe what goes through your body and the rush it (the final whistle) gives you. I don't think you can get it in any other walk of life. It's a sense of fulfilment. There are many times when you work really hard and don't get the rewards but when you do you savour it."

It wasn't all serious po-faced analysis from the trio of Irish players. Kearney spoke about what winning a Grand Slam meant to him and also some of the elder statesmen in the team. He smiled: "It hasn't sunk in but I'll have it for life now, won't I? I'm more delighted for the older lads, the 50 or 60-plus (years of age on the team). They've worked so hard for this."

But it was Bowe who drew peals of laughter when asked had he slept soundly the night before the match. "I slept like a baby! But the craic within the team . . . not many will tell you this, but we tied up the bagman (Rala) in the middle of the night, and sent him down in the lift. We were all sitting there taking photos

GREENWASH IN DAWSON STREET

of this fella going up and down in a glass lift with masking tape over his mouth, and the people in reception didn't know what was going on. But there's a great atmosphere within the squad. You'd think you would be dead nervous, but the belief and the confidence is such that we are able to enjoy ourselves, and then we switch on. The nerves were there today, but we were still able to have a chat, to have the craic but when it comes to it we put the game faces on."

And what of the try? "All through the game I have been asking for a couple of (cross) kicks like that one for the try. There was a lot of space there.

"The ball bounced up perfectly for me but I got a nice whack in the gut from Gav (Henson). I was winded but kept going. I thought 'there must be someone coming across here'. Luckily I made the posts; people jumped on top of me and I couldn't breathe. It was one of those moments where I'd like to have celebrated more, but I couldn't." There'll be plenty of scope for that in the coming weeks and months.

HARRINGTON IMPRESSED BY TEAM'S COOLNESS IN TENSE ENDGAME

23:03:09, MILLENNIUM STADIUM, PHILIP REID

PÁDRAIG HARRINGTON stepped onto a transatlantic flight from Dublin yesterday with an extra spring in his step. The three-time major champion — who is on a seven-week stint to the United States, with the US Masters and his quest for the third leg of the so-called 'Paddy Slam' in the middle of that run of tournaments — knows better than most how sporting endeavours can warm the cockles of a nation's heart and, as an observer this time round, Ireland's Grand Slam win allowed him to wallow in the success of others for a change.

Although he'd attended the Rugby World Cup two years ago and had been offered a ticket to Cardiff for Saturday's match, Harrington chose to watch the game on television at home. "As a sporting occasion, it was fantastic. I'm thrilled for the team, because they have been under a lot of pressure over the years. Fair play to Declan Kidney who has been instrumental in getting the best out of the players and I'm particularly happy to see Brian O'Driscoll get his just rewards," said Harrington.

"The fact they went to Wales and won, that they did things right and worked so hard for each other, makes it even better." What impressed Harrington most about the win over the Welsh was the way the team didn't panic when falling behind to Stephen Jones' drop goal late in the match. "They showed patience and trust, especially in working the play for Ronan's drop goal . . . I obviously don't watch my own stuff when I'm playing, so it was great to sit down and watch the rugby and for us to get the result the whole country wanted," he added.

Charlie Swan, the former champion jockey turned trainer, experienced many fine occasions in his own sporting career - among them the three Champion Hurdles he won on Istabraq - and found the manner of the Grand Slam win to be "nail-biting, it couldn't have been more dramatic." Swan, who watched the match on television with friends, remarked: "It was fantastic, brilliant . . . especially the way it ended when Ronan got that drop goal. The win has given the whole country a lift. We need days like these to get over the doom and gloom, and then Bernard Dunne winning as well. Great."

Briege Corkery, the All Star camogie player and footballer, was similarly enthused. "I thought their determination was great, they way they never gave up. The way they kept going to the end is a lesson for everyone involved in sport, and the win has certainly cheered everyone up." For John O'Mahony, the politician and Mayo football manager, the win was perfectly timed. "People needed a lift and more often than not it comes from sport. This was absolutely fantastic, an exhilarating win and what really impressed me was the unity of purpose with the squad, the team and the management. These players were willing to put their life on the line."

As a two-time All Ireland winning manager in his time with Galway, O'Mahony was extremely impressed with Declan Kidney's input into turning the team into Six Nations champions and Grand Slam achievers. "Listening to Declan Kidney after the match, and the magnanimous way he acknowledged the work that Eddie O'Sullivan did, the honesty of this team came through. I mean, when you hear Paul O'Connell talking about a tackle he missed after the magnificent game he had, it just shows that honesty . . . . this team got what they fully deserved in winning the Grand Slam and they have given the nation a huge lift."

The team's achievement was lauded by Minister for Sport Martin Cullen, who commented: "They are deserving winners of the highest accolade in northern hemisphere rugby and have secured for themselves a permanent place in Irish sporting history . . . huge praise must go to Declan Kidney and his management and coaching team in their first year at the helm and to captain Brian O'Driscoll and all the players for their determination and on an outstanding achievement of which they should all be immensely proud."

TALKING TO THE DUDE

23:03:09, MILLENNIUM STADIUM,
ROSS O'CARROLL KELLY

He's talking to Jack Kyle. The dude's sitting, like, seven or eight rows behind us but the old man is still talking to him.

"History calling," he's going, loud enough for half of Cardiff to hear.

"A date with destiny, full point, new par," and you can see Jack Kyle thinking, 'Er, whatever?'

"Oh, I was there in 48," he tells him, "when we beat this same shower.

"Make no mistake about that. I was still a babe-in-arms of course but my father took me, just as I took this chap here in '82," and he tries to get me to stand up then?

I just shake my arm free and tell him to stop making a tit of himself.

You can see practically half the crowd looking at him, thinking, who is this tosser?

"Bears your name, I'm proud to report - Ross Kyle Gibson McBride O'Carroll-Kelly.

"Described by no less a judge than Tony Ward as the best number 10 never to play for Ireland . . . "

He actually described me as the greatest waste of raw talent he's seen in a half a century watching rugby, but that's a whole other scéal.

"And that little chap beside him there is his own boy - you might say the future of Irish rugby . . . "

Someone eventually shouts, "You, in the leprechaun hat - sit the fock down!" which, thankfully, he does. He asks me what he's missed and I tell him practically the entire first half.

He's there, "Oh, you know what I'm like when I start discussing the greats."

"Who was I named after?" Ronan goes and I know exactly what's he's thinking, because I follow his line of vision to you-know-who, shaping up to take a penalty on the Welsh 10-metre line.

Of course, the easiest thing to do is to tell him what he wants to hear. Except it's, like, complicated between Rog and me? See, a lot of people would be of the opinion that I was the better tactical kicker, the better placekicker, the better basically all-round player. I just liked the life too much and he ended up getting all the breaks. He steps up and pulls his kick wide of the post.

"You were named after Ronan Keating," I go, which is actually true?

"Your mother loved that song Isn't It A Wonder," and I look at his little face and, being honest, he's totally crushed.

But you can't lie to your kids. Anyway, where all this is going is, half-time - you know the script - we're six points down and the old man is telling anyone who's prepared to listen - as well as quite a few who aren't - that what Ireland lack is a kicker of the calibre of Stephen Jones and the great crime, for which the IRFU must stand indicted here today, is that they have one, except he's sitting here in the bloody stand. But the match restarts. Two quick tries and he's suddenly changed his tune.

"The dream is on!" he's going.

I'm telling Ro how Tommy Bowe has been, for me, the revelation of the Six Nations, if that's an actual word. But he's in, like, total awe. He's there, "Did you see Rog's chip over the top, Rosser?" I pull a face like I'm not that impressed? "That's actually not as difficult as it looks," I go, and I feel instantly guilty, because if there's anyone in this stadium who knows what a moment of complete and utter genius that was, it's me. So you know what

JACK KYLE LENDS HIS SUPPORT IN CARDIFF TO THE CLASS OF 2009

happens next. We let Wales back into it and the old man's saying that now is the time for certain individuals to stand up and be counted.

The minutes are disappearing fast. It's, like, ruck after ruck and I'm thinking, now would be a good time for Rog to drop back into the pocket. But I look and of course he's already there. Then the ball is in his hands. And then he's suddenly splitting the posts. I didn't see Stephen Jones's penalty. Ro and the old man didn't either - they had their hands over their eyes. But me, I was just staring at him. See, there are those who say it could and should have been me down there today, but those people are wrong. I could never do what he does and that's a hard thing to admit when you're pushing 30 and someone else is living your dream.

When Jones misses, all hell breaks lose. literally. In all the excitement, I even end up hugging my old man, if you can believe that. He turns around to say something to Jack Kyle but he's gone and you wouldn't focking blame him either. So we end up just sitting there - three generations of us, you could say - staring into space, just emotionally spent.

And I turn to Ro and I go, "You know I was only yanking your chain earlier?" He takes the rollie out of his mouth and looks at me, his little eyes wide. I'm there, "You weren't named after Ronan Keating," and this smile - worth a Grand Slam and two Heineken Cups in anyone's money - just explodes across his face.

DELIVERANCE: SQUAD OF 2009 CLAIM THEIR PLACE IN HISTORY

23:03:09, MILLENNIUM STADIUM, **GERRY THORNLEY**

A NATION expected in these parlous times, and a team delivered. The Irish rugby team removed a 61-year-old monkey from their backs in Cardiff's Millennium Stadium on Saturday with a nerve-shredding, dramatic 17-15 win over Wales to claim a first Grand Slam since 1948, and only Ireland's second in history. The Irish squad returned to Dublin airport yesterday with vice-captain Paul O'Connell carrying the Triple Crown and captain Brian O'Driscoll the Six Nations trophy, as the team having reached its Holy Grail.

On only four occasions since 1948 have an Irish team even reached the last game of the competition with a chance of the Grand Slam. The class of 2009 have, quite simply, completed the greatest achievement in the history of Irish rugby and did so amid the kind of drama that only great sporting theatre can throw up.

Ronan O'Gara's 78th-minute drop goal having regained the lead, television cameras again panned toward Jackie Kyle, the star turn in that sepia-tinged 1948 team, as Welsh outhalf Stephen Jones lined up a 48-metre penalty with the last kick of the game. The ball seemed to hang in the air for an eternity, and was heading towards the Irish posts, before falling just short.

Kyle was one of the estimated 15-20,000 Irish fans among the 74,646 crowd in Cardiff and television viewing figures are likely to break the previous record of 1.2 million for an Irish rugby match. Within an hour of the final whistle, Kyle probably had writer's cramp from signing autographs for emotional Irish fans, many of whom were in tears.

O'Driscoll, probably Ireland's greatest ever rugby player, can expect a similar fate. It was that kind of day, draining, unforgettable and wonderful all at once. President Mary McAleese presented the Six Nations trophy to the team in Cardiff. Yesterday some 2,000 supporters were at the airport to greet the squad before an estimated crowd of 17,500 turned Dawson Street into a sea of green for the Lord Mayor's reception. The heroes of 2009 were then feted in the Mansion House before returning to their hotel. It would be another long night.

AN IMPRESSIVE COLLECTION OF SILVERWARE

HEROES LIFT OUR SPIRITS HIGHER THAN PAUL O'CONNELL IN LINEOUT

23:03:09, MILLENNIUM STADIUM, MIRIAM LORD

HOORAY FOR panic and pleasure and sweet palpitations! Oh, but it did the heart good to feel the heart flutter and skip a beat and almost stop, before the triumphant roar of those brave enough to look made it race again and nearly burst with joy. At long last - a chance to celebrate. Good news, for once. Great news. News to put a smile on your face, and make you sing and cheer and do silly dances. The sort of headline news that has nothing to do with budgets and pay cuts, unemployment figures and politicians' expenses.

The blessed relief of sporting distraction. It didn't matter if you never set eyes upon an oval ball or knotted an old school tie. Whether you are into rugby, soccer, Gaelic, bog-snorkelling or tiddlywinks - it didn't matter. This was a nation responding, admittedly belatedly and in a different fashion, to their Finance Minister's call to "patriotic duty". Thanks to the outdoor exploits of a rugby team and the indoor exploits of a boxer, Ireland grabbed the chance to get out there and party.

On an exhilarating Saturday that stretched giddily into the early hours of Sunday, we broke through the pervading gloom of the last few months and fell happily into the glorious Green beyond. First, a rugby Grand Slam title after a wait of 61 years, and then, the heroic capture of a boxing world title by a courageous Dub with a great line in patter. Gift. Absolutely gift. We're not the better of it yet, thank God.

Bernard Dunne, who was crowned the WBA World super-bantamweight champion in Dublin after a gutsy display of stamina and self-belief saw him knock out the highly rated title-holder, will be honoured by his native city next week. Yesterday belonged to the rugby players. Coach Declan Kidney's team, led by captain Brian O'Driscoll, arrived home at lunchtime and were met by a huge, adoring crowd at Dublin airport. It was a foretaste of what was to come.

Taoiseach Brian Cowen, who has wisely kept out of the limelight during the celebrations, leaving the players to bask in the glory, called into the Mansion House from Government Buildings, where discussions on the economic crisis are ongoing. The Taoiseach, who loves his sport, stood back and applauded with the rest of the guests as the players entered The Round Room. He met the players and looked on proudly as his youngest daughter Meadhbh had her photo taken with O'Driscoll and Ronan O'Gara.

Social Welfare Minister Mary Hanafin, had she been in a line out, would have been penalised for barging as she elbowed her way through the throng to sit beside O'Driscoll and the trophy. If O'Driscoll thought it was tough on the pitch, he didn't reckon on the determination of Irish female politicians. He was sandwiched by Senator Ger Feeney and Cllr Deirdre Heeney, clinging to the trophy for dear life as the rhyming public servants smiled for the camera.

Outside, the crowd waved their green flags and waited for a glimpse of their heroes. Finally, the players emerged from the Mansion House to deafening roars of approval, walking a green carpet and a guard of honour of flagbearers and drummers. Coach Declan Kidney, meanwhile, had a few words with Brian Cowen back inside. Was the Taoiseach asking him the secret of his success? Our IRFU man said that Kidney told his men at half-time that they had been doing everything right, and if they kept that up, the scores would come. "Keep doing what you are doing," he told them. Not, perhaps, the sort of advice to be giving to Brian Cowen.

Jerry Flannery's mother, Jane, was waiting for the son to appear. "I was at the match — there were the Horans and myself and the Hayes. We stayed seated at the end and I swear to God, all the Welsh in front of us stood up. We couldn't see a thing. Then we heard the roar. We thought it was the Welsh roaring, at first, then we realised Ireland had won. There were hugs and kisses and jigs all round." Jerry is one of the many walking wounded on the team. "He has a big, big swollen eye. He needed five stitches," Jane told us, as her son mounted the steps to the platform. She looked on in delight, a proud Irish mother. "And his hair not even combed."

Brian O'Driscoll's girlfriend, actress Amy Huberman, held his nine-month-old niece Aoife in her arms. "I had her on my knee during the game and she hadn't a clue what was happening. Thank God, she was a great distraction. When it was finally over, and I realised we won, I couldn't stop crying for an hour." Tommy Bowe sang a verse of The Black Velvet Band.

At the first sighting of Brian O'Driscoll, the crowd burst into a chorus of "Ole, Ole, Ole." There were high-pitched squeals from the sizable contingent of teenage girls in Ugg boots whenever Ronan O'Gara said or did anything. Then the ticker-tape exploded out of machines at the base of the platform with great gusts of tinselly green. The wind caught the paper and it rained down on the crowd. Sure, it was only a game. Just 80 minutes of diversion. But it was great, and it gladdened the heart and the next few weeks at least will be a little easier and the memories will remain forever. By jingo, isn't patriotism great?

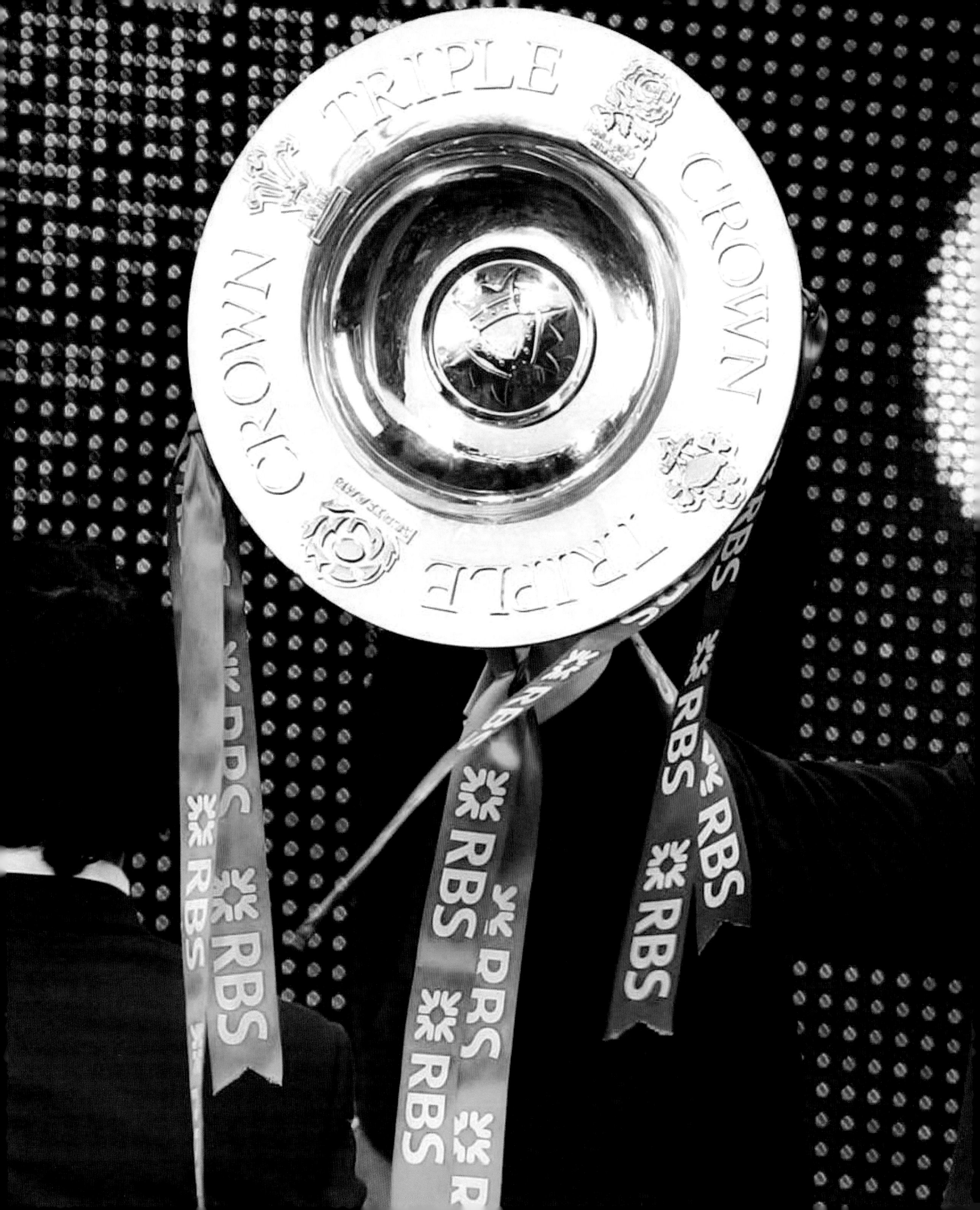
TRIPLE CROWN
TRIPLE CROWN
RBS

DONNCHA O'CALLAGHAN OFFERS SUPPORTERS A CLOSE-UP OF THE TRIPLE CROWN TROPHY.

SEA OF GREEN FLAGS AS TROPHY HELD ALOFT IN DUBLIN HOMECOMING

23:03:09, DUBLIN, **MARIE O'HALLORAN**

DUBLIN CITY centre was a sea of green yesterday as up to 20,000 supporters packed in and around Dawson Street to welcome home the Six Nations' Champions. Ecstatic fans waved a sea of green flags outside the Mansion House while hundreds more watched proceedings on a giant screen on St Stephen's Green. Crowds started gathering around 1pm but had to wait until almost 4.30pm before their heroes made it on stage in front of the Lord Mayor's mansion. But the wait turned into something of a gig as they were entertained by rock band Jungle Boogie.

Meanwhile politicians, family members, friends and other dignitaries gathered in the Mansion House Round room for a reception, among them Taoiseach Brian Cowen. "When the ref put his hand up for the last penalty British-Irish relations were at stake," he quipped to reporters. Minister for Social and Family Affairs Mary Hanafin said of the team "I don't think they realise what they've done for the mood of the country".

The golden boys themselves arrived by bus to the back entrance of the Mansion House. They were welcomed by deputy Lord Mayor Cllr Emer Costello, who said "how proud we are of your achievement" and "you are simply the best". IRFU president John Lyons, who described the team as having a "never say die" spirit, said "we're on a sort of odyssey" that started for captain Brian O'Driscoll at the under-19 World Cup in Toulouse.

Brian himself described the journey to victory as "a long, long quest". They held to the mantra "never give up" and in the end "managed to sneak it".

On the way out to the waiting crowds, forward Donncha O'Callaghan described the event as a "huge honour," before adding, "if we didn't win yesterday we'd have scarred an awful lot of players," he said with a huge grin.

On the street the match highlights were rerun on big screens, to tumultous cheers. RTÉ's Des Cahill welcomed the management on stage and then the team. In groups they came out the Mansion House door, down the green carpet through a guard of honour who played drums and waved green flags, and up on stage amid huge applause.

Paul O'Connell described the most memorable part of the Wales match. "The last five minutes of the game was something. Two drop goals and the last kick - that they missed." Ronan O'Gara, asked his thoughts when the Welsh got the last minute penalty said "I was ready to kill Paddy" who gave away the penalty. Paddy himself quipped: "I just felt the game lacked a bit of excitement."

Then Brian O'Driscoll and coach Declan Kidney arrived on stage to tumultous applause, and a rousing chorus of "Olé, olé, olé". O'Driscoll told the crowd it was all "fantastic" and "when you wake up in the morning you're not as sore as you would be if you'd lost". Declan Kidney spoke of the last five minutes of the game and "as in any game you play to the 80th minute".

Try-scorer Tommy Bowe, forced into singing the chorus of Black Velvet Band, was the master of understatement in describing his score as "nice". Then the moment everyone waited for arrived. Brian O'Driscoll and Declan Kidney held up the Six Nations'Trophy to rapturous applause, as green confetti was released into the sky. The PA system belted out U2's "In The Name of Love". Perhaps "There'll be Days like This" might better have described the mood.

YOUNG AND OLD COME TOGETHER TO ACCLAIM THE IRISH SQUAD

WALES

WRU

15 **LEE BYRNE** (Ospreys)
14 **MARK JONES** (Scarlets)
13 **TOM SHANKLIN** (Cardiff)
12 **GAVIN HENSON** (Ospreys)
11 **SHANE WILLIAMS** (Ospreys)
10 **STEPHEN JONES** (Scarlets)
9 **MIKE PHILLIPS** (Ospreys)
1 **GETHIN JENKINS** (Cardiff)
2 **MATTHEW REES** (Scarlets)
3 **ADAM JONES** (Ospreys)
4 **IAN GOUGH** (Ospreys)
5 **ALUN-WYN JONES** (Ospreys)
6 **DAFYDD JONES** (Scarlets)
7 **MARTYN WILLIAMS** (Cardiff)
8 **RYAN JONES** (Ospreys)

REPLACEMENTS
Jamie Roberts (Cardiff) for Byrne (31 mins)
Huw Bennett (Ospreys) for Rees (56 mins)
Luke Charteris (Dragons) for Gough (56 mins)

NOT USED
John Yapp (Cardiff)
Jonathan Thomas (Ospreys)
Wayne Fury (London Irish)
James Hook (Ospreys)

15-17

S Jones pen	36:16
S Jones pen	42:13
	H-T
	3:28 O'Driscoll try
	5:17 O'Gara con
	6:47 Bowe try
	7:56 O'Gara con
S Jones pen	12:36
S Jones pen	17:55
S Jones drop	41:11
	44:45 O'Gara drop

IRELAND

ROB KEARNEY (Leinster) 15
TOMMY BOWE (Ospreys) 14
BRIAN O'DRISCOLL (Leinster, capt) 13
GORDON D'ARCY (Leinster) 12
LUKE FITZGERALD (Leinster) 11
RONAN O'GARA (Munster) 10
TOMÁS O'LEARY (Munster) 9
MARCUS HORAN (Munster) 1
JERRY FLANNERY (Munster) 2
JOHN HAYES (Munster) 3
DONNCHA O'CALLAGHAN (Munster) 4
PAUL O'CONNELL (Munster) 5
STEPHEN FERRIS (Ulster) 6
DAVID WALLACE (Munster) 7
JAMIE HEASLIP (Leinster) 8

REPLACEMENTS
Denis Leamy (Munster) for Ferris (7 mins)
Tom Court (Ulster) for Hayes (23-27 mins)
Rory Best (Ulster) for Flannery (67 mins)
Geordan Murphy (Leicester) for Kearney (67mins)
Peter Stringer (Munster) for O'Leary (68 mins)
Paddy Wallace (Ulster) for Fitzgerald (76 mins)

NOT USED
Mick O'Driscoll (Munster)

Six Nations Championship: Final standing

	P	W	D	L	F	A	Pts
IRELAND	5	5	0	0	121	73	10
England	5	3	0	2	124	70	6
France	5	3	0	2	124	101	6
Wales	5	3	0	2	100	81	6
Scotland	5	1	0	4	79	102	2
Italy	5	0	0	5	49	170	0

ITALY **8** FRANCE **50**

ENGLAND **26** SCOTLAND **12**

Millennium Stadium, March 21st, 2009. Attendance: 74,645
Referee Wayne Barnes (England)
Touch judge Dave Pearson (England) Stuart Terheege (England)
TMO Romain Poite (France)

THE INSIDE TRACK
DUBLIN, MARCH

As the sun shone brightly on Sunday, March 22nd, Irish rugby basked in the warm glow. There had never been a season like it and, quite possibly, there may never be again. On that morning, the Grand Slam, the Six Nations and the Triple Crown were all Irish owned, and, almost as gloriously, Leinster and Munster would go on to ensure that the Heineken Cup and the Magners League followed.

An Irishman, Paul O'Connell, would captain an original record selection of 14 Irishmen on the Lions' trip to South Africa. While that was going on, even the Churchill Cup (the one we always wanted!) would fall into Irish possession for the first time when an Ireland A team coached by the Kidney Brains Trust, and featuring nine players who were not regular starters with their provinces, beat an England Saxons team of players who were regular starters in the Guinness Premiership, by 49-22 in Denver, Colorado. Lock, stock and barrel, the whole shooting gallery, was now in the possession of Irish rugby.

This is the inside story of 24 hours in Cardiff that delivered one of the greatest triumphs in Irish sporting history.

SATURDAY, 21ST MARCH:
WALES V IRELAND, CYMRU V IWERDDON, CARDIFF.

8.30AM-10.30AM. BREAKFAST, THE HILTON HOTEL

Breakfast was a looser affair than normal on a match day, due to a later kick-off of 5.30pm. Most of the training, preparation and work had been done by Thursday. There wasn't much more to be said or done, all the more so as this match came at the end of an intense, five game, seven weekend odyssey. During that period Kidney had been acutely conscious of the need to reduce training and afford players breaks from the camp and, come match day, not to overload them. That week, less was more. The emphasis was on rest and eating.

"I'd say I was up at 10.29am," jokes Peter Stringer, who had roomed with David Wallace and therefore stayed up late.

"The usual, probably couldn't get to bed before 1.00am. We'd been up at 7.45am or 8.0am all week because of meetings and training. The morning of the day before the game and the day of the game are the two mornings when you can get a bit of a lie-in."

Most had finished their breakfast, and were sitting around having a coffee and chatting. Stringer likes to have his porridge on a match day.

"It sets you up really well, along with some scrambled eggs and beans along with a protein shake. I like to eat a good meal in the morning so you don't have to force yourself to eat a big meal later in the day. You could be on after two minutes and you have to have that approach but I was quite relaxed considering the occasion. I've been that way in the last couple of months in my approach to games. I was thinking to myself `should I be more nervous?'"

Jerry Flannery roomed with Tomás O'Leary, and they didn't descend for breakfast until about 10.45am.

"I actually enjoy match day," says Flannery. "It's a day when you only have to think about one thing. You get up, have your breakfast, go back to bed and sleep or I might read a bit of a book."

Gordon D'Arcy roomed with Luke Fitzgerald, who was up and gone by 7.45am D'Arcy tried to get back to sleep, couldn't, so went down for breakfast and back to bed.

"It was a very quiet morning. I like to go out for a cup of coffee on the morning of a game but it was too busy. So I had to grab coffee and went to the team room. But it's not the same really."

"I sleep in, I go over notes early and I always try to find a walk and a coffee away from the hotel," says Les Kiss, the defensive coach. "That was the first time my wife, Julie, was over, so we went for a coffee together."

Gert Smal had been through a World Cup final day, so was also quite relaxed.

"It's a very nice coaching group, pretty much the same as we had with the Boks. Normally we'd already have been planning for the next week's match, but, as this was the last game, I took the opportunity to go to the gym and have a good work-out. I hadn't been to the gym for quite some time and it was good to get rid of the nerves. It doesn't matter what you've coached before you still have nerves, and if you didn't have those butterflies there's probably something wrong. Then I got my filing sorted out."

As Padraig Harrington had explained to them before Christmas, the trick is to keep the right side of their brains, ie the feminine side, relatively uncluttered. Not dissimilarly to this Irish squad, Harrington had been perceived as something of a nearly man on the back of so many second-placed finishes before winning three majors in two years. Harrington spoke of his mental approach to the majors and developing a winning attitude, and his attitude towards mistakes and disappointments.

"What I liked about him was that he was just so honest," says Flannery. "It wasn't just a 'spiel' he was coming out with. I felt like I kinda got to know him. You don't realise the groundwork that was put in then but you look back now and you realise it really did make a difference."

Perhaps this contributed to the relatively relaxed atmosphere on match days, even on Grand Slam match day. Stringer and Donncha O'Callaghan went to the team room to watch Soccer AM. The Welsh rugby squad undertook the Crossbar Challenge.

"A good way to relax and kill a few hours," says Stringer. "They probably weren't as accurate as soccer teams might have been," he adds diplomatically.

Frank O'Driscoll and his wife, Geraldine, had struck up a deep friendship with the parents of Dwayne Peel, and in return for them having stayed with the O'Driscolls for the Croke Park game in 2008, they were due to return the favour on this occasion.

"Very sadly," recalls O'Driscoll Snr, "Dwayne's sister lost a baby at 20 weeks the week of the game, so they were in a terrible state and we decided to find a hotel. Luckily we found accommodation."

They stayed in the Novotel on Schooner Way, a 15-minute walk to the ground but off the main thoroughfare and away from the madding crowds. But that didn't help too much.

"We found the stress coming up to this game almost unbearable," admits O'Driscoll Snr. "We thought as we were getting older we'd get better but in fact we're getting worse. And the 5.30pm kick-off makes the day very long."

In the Novotel, they met the Peels, Denis and Maria, and then their own daughters Julie and Susan, along with Julie's husband Tomas and their two children Katie (two and a half) and Aoife (nine months). Both were in baby sized Irish jerseys.

12.30PM. TO EAT OR NOT TO EAT, THAT IS THE QUESTION

Lunch, as such, or a snack. Some, such as Flannery, skipped it, whereas Stringer opted to eat some chicken and pasta there and then, knowing that he'd struggle to force it down later.

"I could barely eat, and forced some pasta and potatoes," admits D'Arcy. "Normally I've the constitution of an ox but you just go with the flow of the day."

2.00PM. OFFICIAL DUTIES

Kidney conducted a brief meeting about the referee and the weather forecast, with some 'power points' from Mervyn Murphy.

The squad then took their traditional walkabout through an underground tunnel for some fresh air across the road from the hotel at a green area outside the walls of the park. A crowd of Irish and Welsh supporters begin to gather above on the footpath and watch, but without being intrusive.

"We've been playing this game every week, Biscuit Ball," says Flannery. "Backs against forwards. The two teams line up facing each other, side by side, with your hands behind your back. Only one guy can go for the ball. It's always a good laugh. It's better than going out to do lineouts. It keeps it laid back."

Smal is content to just walk through what he calls their 'contest systems' on the opposition ball, having altered their approach to do most of the work earlier in the week.

"There's not much more you can do. You just try to touch the right buttons when you're talking to individuals, and it's important that you as a coaching staff also look composed and calm, otherwise it rubs off on the players if you look nervous."

On match days, he likes the players to 'actualise' what they're going to do, without too much interference from him.

"Gert Smal stopped it (doing lineouts) on the day of the game," says Flannery. "At the start of the Six Nations we did absolutely tons of them, an insane amount of them, but early in the week. If we've weights on a Monday, we do lineouts straight after. We'd have lineouts again on the Tuesday

JAMIE HEASLIP GIVES ADAM JONES A HAIR-RAISING EXPERIENCE

and we worked on the basis that by match day you've all your work done."

"The backs won convincingly yet again," says Stringer of the "Biscuit Ball". "It was nearly a whitewash over the whole campaign bar one which the forwards won."

"No I don't think so," says Flannery. "I think the backs cheat a lot. It's just poorly reffed."

"We won again," says D'Arcy, "and the forwards have more players."

The latter account is verified by Kiss.

"The backs won fair and square. If there was any cheating they were all at it."

2.30PM. PRE-MATCH MEAL

Flannery loads up with some spaghetti Bolognese, chicken and potatoes.

"It took me a while to eat it, but I knew it was going to be a long hard game."

D'Arcy remembers saying that thank God they'd got to this stage.

"Over the previous 24 hours each hour seemed to take longer. The four hours until we got onto the bus seemed to drag by. You savour what happens after but not before. I made a new play list, I was that bored. When I sat down, I wanted to stand up. I packed my bag for the next day, which I normally never do."

The players returned to their rooms and pack for the game.

"That's the time we start focussing on the game," says Stringer. "What I normally do is get an old notepad and pen, go through everything in your head, each position on the pitch, the different moves, be it scrum or lineout, different calls, and write it all down on a bit of paper just to refresh the mind, and you'd bring that on the bus with you. It's like being back in school and the fear of an exam, that horrible feeling that you mightn't have done enough. But I think there was a general feeling that guys were well prepared and we'd done our work."

3.50PM. THE SQUAD ASSEMBLE FOR A BRIEF ADDRESS BY KIDNEY

"It's quite a good feeling when the boys sit around in that circle, with Declan in amongst them," says Kiss. "The rest of the staff sit behind them. None of the players said anything. They were ticking along. Declan picks his little themes, and to make sure that we didn't leave anything for when we look in the mirror afterwards."

4.0PM-4.05PM. SHORT JOURNEY ESCORTED BY TWO MOUNTED POLICEWOMEN

Flannery noted the contrast from a Heineken Cup final, when he could feed off the massed thousands of the Red Army and enjoy it. This time it was mostly red again, but Welsh.

"Some lads stay in the dressingroom and read the programme or something," says D'Arcy. "I like to go out and kick a ball at the crossbar, then I go back inside, get a rub, and then I do a run around for six or seven minutes, with someone else if they want to or on my own. Everyone does their own thing."

4.35PM. BRIAN O'DRISCOLL ATTENDS THE TOSS

On arrival at the ground, O'Driscoll's parents met the O'Garas and others.

"Joan O'Gara informed me that she felt really good and that we were going to win. And I never saw her so positive in my life," Frank smiled.

They usually end up sitting in the general location of the other parents. If there were any regrets amongst some of the players it was that some of those who had played through much of the Noughties and the many near misses were no longer part of the team, in particular the popular Malcolm O'Kelly, who had been Ireland's most capped player of all time entering the Six Nations. But after the opening two matches, he had been jettisoned from the squad altogether for some timekeeping issues and replaced by Mick O'Driscoll. On this Saturday morning of March 21st, O'Kelly was presenting medals along with Denis Hickie to underage players at Templeville Road, home ground of St Mary's.

"We missed the Horgans, the Dempseys and the O'Kellys," admits Frank O'Driscoll. "They had been with us for so long, and we felt there was a chunk missing. We used to hang around and go for meals, and still do at Leinster games. We could have anything from ten to 16 or 18 people at dinner. It was just a pity that they weren't there for this one, but they were certainly there in spirit with us."

4.55PM. THE WARM-UP

Paul Pook, who had taken over from Mike McGurn as the squad's fitness and conditioning coach, begins the warm-up, which is co-ordinated by Kidney and has been condensed into 22 or 23 minutes with almost military precision. It's one of the noisier stadiums pre-match, and at the team meeting on the Thursday Kidney deliberately had his delivery interrupted by the Welsh national anthem blaring in the room.

"We're kind of used to it in Munster," Flannery chuckles, "but maybe some of the other lads were wondering what was going on. It might seem silly but if it means one fella is not shaken by it when he's in the ground then it's worth doing."

Doing a ruck clearout drill, Flannery hit Denis Leamy and suffered a 'stinger' down his right side.

"I went over to the physio and tried to get the feeling back in my right shoulder. The forwards went to do lineouts; I could see Rory throwing the ball and I thought 'oh no'. But I managed to run over and it didn't lock up. I couldn't feel it a bit during the game but it was okay. In that intensity, you don't have time to think about it.

"I'd say we dropped the first four balls (of the warm-up)," recalls D'Arcy, "but for some reason it didn't worry me. I was more worried about myself. My legs felt really, really heavy."

Kiss, like Pook and Smal, had put out the cones for his short, pre-match defence drill. Kidney likes to go out onto the pitch and toss some grass in the air at various points to check out the wind. While Smal is overseeing a couple of lineouts and some cleanout work with the forwards, Gaffney is taking the backs.

"I'm usually the second last bit," says Kiss. "They've usually got the blood pumping and we try to set a tone, it's not about technique. We just had two hits each shoulder into the pads and try to work in unison in terms of getting up the line. Then Declan takes them for two plays up and down the field to finish it."

5.18PM. COUNTDOWN TO THE KICK-OFF

Kidney especially, Smal, Kiss and Gaffney talk to the players individually and in groups, giving the last words of encouragement or trigger points. "But that's usually a player-led thing," said Kiss. "This is when the hype is cranked up. A lot of special words are said between the players, led by Brian and Paul."

"It was a very nice vibe, there was good talk before the game," says Smal. "In fact I like the way the Irish build up to the game compared to the way we (South Africa) do it. Sometimes I think we're too quiet in the dressingroom."

The kick-off had been put back three minutes because of the lengthy treatment for Harry Ellis in the England-Scotland game. Paul McNaughton kept them up to date on the wall under the clock in the dressingroom, writing 'three minute delay'.

"A lot of stuff is stuff that has to be said every time," admits Flannery. "Certain defensive things, or watch for so-and-so's left foot step."

But O'Connell spoke of going out to try and win the game.

"Certain little points stick with you," says Flannery, "and I thought 'jeez, yeah, we have to go out and win this game. Instead of thinking we could lose a Grand Slam, I was thinking in my head we would have the mentality of going to Wales to spoil their party. And when Paulie said that it really hit home. There's no point in going out trying to contain them."

The players bounced up and down in a circle. The last words. Stringer and the subs put on their tops, forming a small tunnel to clap the starting XV out, then take their positions at the end of the line for the anthems before returning to their allotted seats. And the mantra ringing in their ears was O'Connell's.

"We are unbreakable. We are unbreakable."

When the players have left the dressingroom, the stillness is marked. The coaches are led by McNaughton to the lift for their box in the stands. As Kiss puts it: "I think it was Guus Hiddink who said 'Monday to Friday are coaches' days but that diminishes as each day goes by, and Saturday is players' day. And that's exactly what it is. You feel confident you've done enough preparation but you still have questions in your mind. But the smartest thing you can sometimes decide on as a coach is what you leave out."

THE NATIONAL ANTHEMS

"You grow up watching games when you're young and you almost look forward to the other national anthems," says Flannery. "I always love hearing the Welsh and Scottish national anthems. It's not really intimidating. It almost reminds you of when you were younger."

WELSH SECOND ROW IAN GOUGH CAN'T STOP GORDON D'ARCY

5.35 KICK-OFF

Ireland's game plan centred around field position. The more minutes they played in the Welsh half the more it would ultimately tell, pushing to the corners or putting up a high ball, trying to keep Wales under as much pressure as possible.

"It was quite a simple thing the way Declan delivered it," says Kiss.

Whereas the coaches are higher up in the stand, the replacements look on from pitchside.

"It's not a great vantage point," says Stringer. "It's below pitch level nearly, and I know I'm below the level of everyone else at the best of times, with people walking in front of you. You want to see the game and analyse it. You're hoping to get on and you'd like to see how Wales are defending."

The replacements went for a couple of stretches behind one goal, and lingered there longer than normal simply because it was a better viewing point. D'Arcy's first flat pass from O'Driscoll allowed him to step inside Tom Shanklin after Gavin Henson had broken the line and left a hole.

"That settled me in," says D'Arcy. "We knew they couldn't blitz if we got quick ball, so while it was kinda off the cuff it was also programmed as well."

About four minutes in O'Leary's pass inadvertently teed up Flannery for a huge hit by Ian Gough.

"I was shouting to Tomás `this is on'. They'd missed whoever was inside me, and I was thinking if I get this quickly I can cut back inside and straighten up fast. But I had to check and Gough lined me up. I was pissed off because that's a big lift for them."

Even so, generally Ireland had one of their better starts. In defence, they were out-blitzing the blitzers. Gradually too, they were contesting well on the Welsh throw, with O'Connell making telling inroads.

"I was quite chuffed with most things," admits Flannery. "One or two scrums weren't good enough but the lineouts went well. Our contesting was good, especially when Donncha got that first ball, and Paul picked up from that. The only thing was our hit (in the scrum) wasn't good enough. That was one thing I spoke about at half-time, and the hit was a little bit better."

"The Welsh have a good pack," admits Smal, "a fairly heavy pack and a good scrummaging pack. They even gave the All Blacks a hard time. Still, I'm not satisfied with our scrum. I think it can improve quite a bit, but that will come in time. We have to manage our players, but in the future we'll address that more aggressively."

SHARP PRACTICE

Smal was disappointed that more didn't come from the lineout steals, all the more so as the referee, Wayne Barnes, missed O'Connell being played in the air. Right enough, after a couple of steals, Alun-Wyn Jones can be seen tugging him by the shoulder and the jersey in making O'Connell land awkwardly.

"But they were at sixes and sevens there, which was a big part of the game where we beat them," adds the South African.

"It's attritional the way we play," admits Flannery. "We need to be a little more clinical in the way we execute our play, but that's us evolving as a team. One of the things we talked about was making the pitch small for them; never getting isolated and constantly talking in defence, constantly building trees with the two lads beside you. No one was getting isolated because we know that they like to play with a massive tempo and if somebody switches off we know that Shane Williams, Lee Byrne or whoever will isolate someone, use their footwork, and get an offload or beat them."

Nearing half-time, Stephen Jones landed a monster penalty, his second. It was a good half everywhere except on the scoreboard.

"To be zero at half-time was unusual," admits Kiss, "but that's one of the qualities that's come through in this team; the way they come through. And at half-time we felt this was in our pocket if we did the right things in the second half."

An abiding memory for Flannery was O'Connell being hit with a no arm tackle by Gough and carrying on, shouting at the ref as he did so. In virtually the last play of the half.

"Gough then got me with a no arm tackle. Well it felt like a no arm tackle," says Flannery. "That bust up my eye. Maybe I need to work on my footwork so I'm not running into brick walls."

In fact, in the aftermath of the game Flannery rang the Munster conditioning coach Tom Cummins, and did some footwork drills on Wednesday and Thursday!

D'Arcy went to the dressing-room "knowing that there was more in the tank even though I was giving everything that I had." He would speak to Shanklin later that evening. "He said they were really happy at half-time but we were really happy at half-time as well."

HALF-TIME: WALES 6 IRELAND 0

Kidney spoke first, then Kiss, before the players broke up into units. Flannery had to go to the medical room for seven stitches above his left eye. "When I came back Gert (Smal) was talking to the pack and was saying lineouts are going well but to get a little bit more aggressive in the scrum and get the hits through."

It was also mentioned that Wales weren't quite as aggressive in defence as had been anticipated and trained for, and that O'Gara and the backs could afford to attack a little bit flatter, put the ball in front of each other.

"The right things said and the right things not said," says Kiss. "One of the defining things for me was that we definitely knew that in each game we could lift the tempo going into the second half. And I think that's a quality to do with being fresh and the way that Declan managed the whole campaign. The players didn't over train."

Smal adds: "There's a huge amount of character and spirit in the team, so that they can lift it when they need to. If we can get our mindset right, especially with the talent we have in this team, we can go places."

O'Driscoll had the final, telling say. Powerfully getting his message across, he said that they were where they wanted to be and he spoke of the complete belief he had in his team-mates, in everything about the squad and that they would be the stronger team as the game went on.

WELSH OUTHALF STEPHEN JONES WATCHES HIS LAST GASP PENALTY DROP SHORT

THE SECOND-HALF

The Irish game plan is to keep going at teams in the belief that they will eventually wilt.

"Wales are a bit like Wasps, they believe that they are fitter than everyone else," says Flannery. "I remember talking to Redser (Eoin Reddan) in the build-up to the game and how they play exactly like Wasps. When the ball goes to touch, Lee Byrne would take a quick lineout to himself and all the Welsh guys would go 'yes, we're going to kill them now.' And we were saying how we could turn that to our advantage, how when the Welsh boys go 'yes' they would see us go past them in a line, never getting tired, and maybe eventually they'd go: 'why aren't these guys folding?' It was like a dream few minutes. Marcus Horan made a great point to me subsequently. When we got that first try we worked so hard for it and it was exactly how we envisaged scoring. For Tommy's try it barely seemed like we had to do anything. Then you walk back and think 'that was easy'. And then I think we stopped playing a little."

"I remember shouting at Brian (O'Driscoll) just before he went in there (among the forwards), 'why are you ****ing going in there?'" admits D'Arcy. "But he didn't listen to me at all, thankfully."

Spare a thought for the parents, for whom the game must have been unbearable. The O'Driscolls watched the dramatic events alongside Anne Bowe and the Kearneys, with the O'Garas in front of them and the D'Arcys, Horans, O'Connells and Wallaces in the general vicinity, although they were all a bit scattered around as usual.

"Only when it was announced," did Frank O'Driscoll realise his son had scored the first try. "The only good thing I have to say about the referee (Wayne Barnes) is that he was one of the few guys in the ground that spotted the try."

HOMEWORK

Mervyn Murphy's video analysis had revealed that Shane Williams liked to defend 'up and in' off opposition scrums. Alan Gaffney and Mark Tainton hatched a plan, the players practiced O'Gara's 'kick pass to Tommy Bowe' off a scrum assiduously, all of it driven cleverly by Kidney.

"They just shaped it beautifully with the players," says Kiss.

"When you practice something all week and it comes off on the pitch, it's so nice," says D'Arcy, "and Rog was putting his kicks on the money."

Gradually though, as Barnes' second half penalty count went 8-1 to Wales, the home side inched their way back with two more Stephen Jones penalties to make it 14-12.

"They never looked like scoring a try really but we kept them in it with penalties," says D'Arcy. "That's the most penalties we've given away in the whole tournament. He did me twice for holding on and I just couldn't believe it. I was amazed by some of his decisions."

"I thought the penalty for pushing was a bit pedantic," says Kiss in relation to the reversed penalty against Donncha O'Callaghan with which Jones made it 14-12. "I guess if we'd lost we'd be blowing up big time."

"I undercooked Paulie on a lob with my last throw and Alun Wyn-Jones stole it: I was kinda disappointed with that," said Flannery, "but in general I thought it (the Irish lineout) was pretty good and the boys did a bit of a number on theirs. You come off and I tried to detach myself as much as I could, or else the next 13 minutes were going to drive me bananas."

UP IN THE COACHES' BOX

"It's interesting, it's not like it's a structured operation," says Kiss. "Sometimes you say something and someone says something back." The Australian continued: "But it's not like a play station game where you can control it. As much as you think you can put messages out, sometimes they just go nowhere. You're probably just pleasing yourself as a coach by putting something out most of the time."

"It's quite nerve-wracking watching and not being able to do anything," says Stringer. "You become a tremendous critic on the bench as well, because you can see things so much clearer, but you also have the understanding and appreciation as to how physical it is out on the pitch, and that holds you back."

About 12 or 13 minutes from the end of the match, physio Brian Greene informed Stringer that he was to go on and, as he stood up, Murphy told him that he was going on at the next break of play in the Welsh half. That happened 30 or 40 seconds later.

"If there isn't an injury you're kinda preparing yourself to come on around the 60 or 70 minute mark. I suppose there are two different approaches. In this game we were two points ahead and you were going out with the attitude not to lose the game and not do anything stupid that might lose us the match. If you're coming on trying to win a game from behind you've a totally different mental approach."

Mike Philips made his first break of the championship.

"I got back and, I think, got hold of one of his legs and tried to drag him down," says Stringer. "He's a big unit."

STEPHEN JONES' DROP GOAL MAKES IT 15-14 TO WALES

"Normally I try and get a charge on a drop goal but he didn't drop back into the pocket," says Stringer. "There's that kind of sinking feeling in your stomach when you go behind and there's only five minutes left. But you banish the doubts in your head fairly quickly. The next target is to get hold of the ball and get back down there."

"I wasn't that worried," maintains Flannery. "We know what we have to do to score and it's worked for us in the past. I knew if we got down there and got possession, we'd get a chance."

"It's grand, we've got five minutes here," D'Arcy thought. "We'll get a drop goal in five minutes, easy. We'll get two if we need it."

O'GARA'S DROP GOAL

Stringer kept barking, notably at a momentarily prone Marcus Horan.

"I know they're fucked at that stage, but if you're on the ground yourself and you hear someone encouraging you it nearly snaps you out of that momentary daze when you're so physically exhausted. The forwards had worked really hard at keeping possession and I just felt with all eight forwards there we could work them infield closer to the posts with a few pick and gos - keep the forwards as tight as possible. Once we got close to the posts I looked up and saw Rory Best run in front of Rog. I had to hold it a second and then Paulie went in front of me. I saw the Welsh defence ready to push up and basically I just hit Rog with the pass, and he did his thing again."

"They (the Welsh) were really on me so I really had to get the ball up - it was ugly but it flew straight and that's all that matters," said O'Gara. "But it was 90 seconds too early - we gave them another shot."

"There was an unbreakable belief," says Kiss, "and even though the second half penalty count was 8-1 and he didn't' ref them the same as he reffed us, the kicking game and the pressure points kept building slowly and they came to fruition. The way it all worked just says volumes for where they'd come as a group. It was special, to say the least. You just can't say enough about temperament that people have in those moments."

Flannery and the rest of the Irish squad on the sidelines were happy.

"This is just such a sweet way to finish it all off," Flannery thought to himself. "A few more minutes and we'll be celebrating on the field."

"I was flabbergasted how he O'Gara was able to lift it up over their arms," says O'Driscoll Snr "because he was adamant that they were miles offside, and they looked it. But then I thought of the re-start against France when it wasn't fielded," he adds, in reference to the Vincent Clerc try at Croke Park two years before which ultimately denied Ireland a Grand Slam and Championship.

THE JONES PENALTY

"I didn't expect that last penalty," admits Smal. "That took the wind out of me. It was a huge flip of emotions."

"I turned to my wife and said 'this is it'. I do not believe this," says O'Driscoll, "and for the first time in my life I put my head down. She couldn't look at it either."

"I was sick to my stomach. I just felt he was going to slot it easily, like a lot of other people as well," admits Stringer.

"I was in another ruck, got up and saw it was a penalty," recalls D'Arcy. "What happened lads? But I was relieved to see Jones taking it. I just didn't think he had it in him at that point in the game. The 80th minute of a seriously tough game in hot conditions. I still couldn't watch. If you look at the video I'm behind the post with my head on the padding. I heard a cheer and thought '***, he's got it'. But then it wasn't a huge cheer," D'Arcy adds. "That's an Irish cheer. I heard Geordie and Rog calling for it. I saw Geordie catch it and I remember screaming at him to kick it out. I looked at the referee. Yeeeesssss."

"I would have backed Jones to put it over. I would have backed Henson even more," says Flannery. "When he took the kick I couldn't see it clearly. It looked like it had the legs and then it just died. I just saw Paulie's arms going out and him running, and then I was out on the field."

"I thought the kick was going over, I saw it on target and thought we'd lost it," admitted O'Connell, who within moments would, memorably, be running like a lunatic from the pitch, arms raised skywards. "It went from losing the whole thing to winning the whole thing in half a second."

"My heart goes out to Stephen really, the game also meant so much to him." admitted O'Gara, who was to rival Jones for the Lions number 10

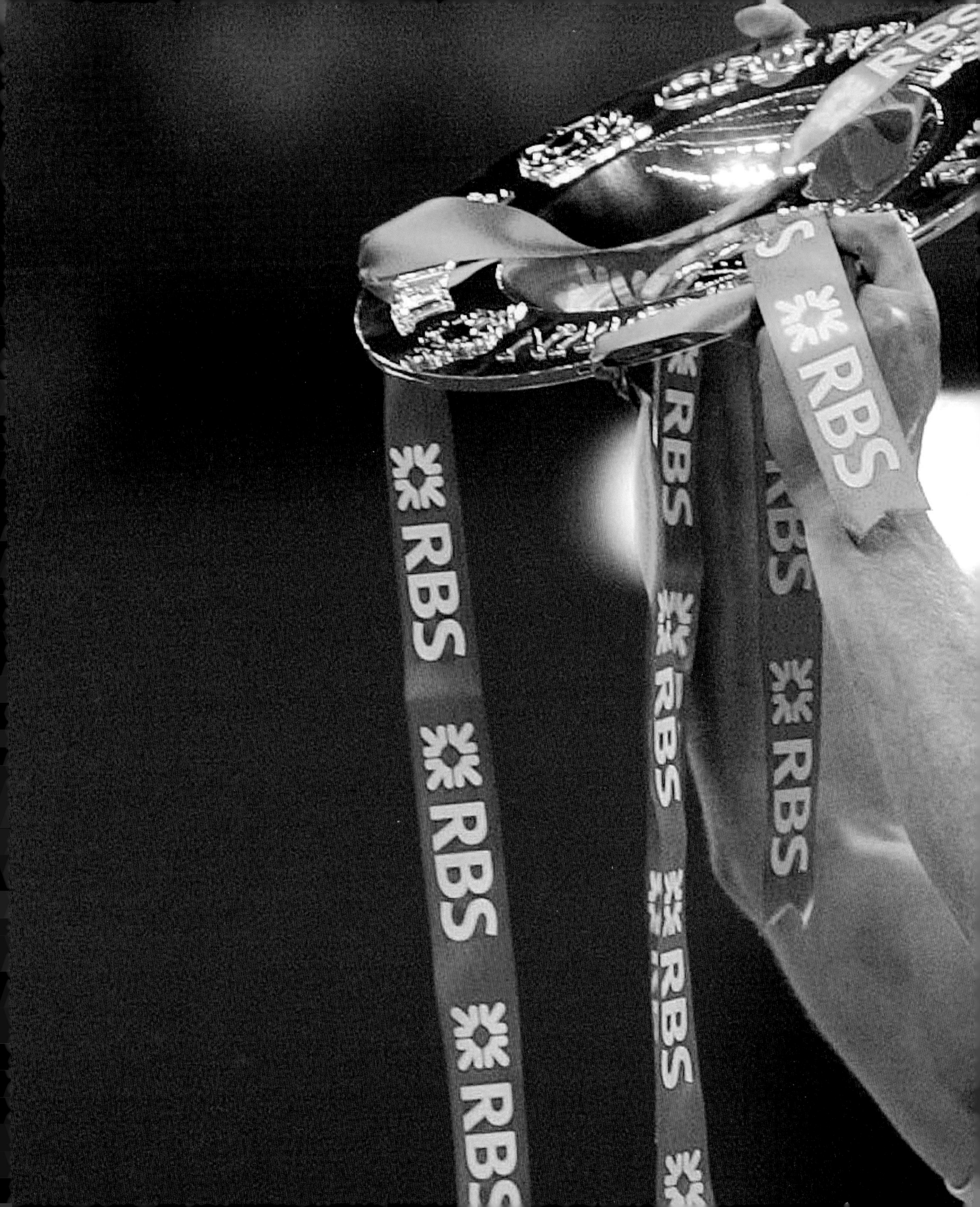
RBS

PAUL O'CONNELL WITH THE TRIPLE CROWN TROPHY

jersey in the summer. Immediately he consoled his opposite number and rashly exchanged jerseys. "It's so unfair the pressure all comes down to the kickers. I just wanted to console with him and congratulate him on a good game. I know Stephen well enough that I might get my shirt back for a few quid!"

Up in the coaches' box, Kiss, Smal and Tainton stood up to watch the kick but Kidney told them to sit down.

"A lot of people said we looked calm but we were churning on the inside," laughs Kiss. "I watched the boys jumping on the pitch for three to five seconds, which was wonderful, then turned for some high fives and we all suddenly enveloped into a group hug. A bit of man love. It doesn't hurt, does it?"

MANLY TEARS

"That coaching box exploded," admits Smal. "That's why you coach rugby, to have those sort of feelings. That's probably the time when you get rid of all your frustrations, in a nice way. It brought a lump to our throats, and maybe a tear to the eye."

"I heard a cheer and looked up, and the next thing I saw was Geordan running sideways with the ball," says O'Driscoll Snr. "I said 'oh my god it didn't go over'. Then I saw him kick it into the stands and at that stage we went berserk. Everybody hugged and we were 'lepping' up and down. All I could think of were the guys out on the pitch who had been trying for this for most of the last ten years. They finally had this monkey off their backs, and the other thing was the unbelievable graciousness of the Welsh, even within a minute. But I don't know if I'd like to go through the stress again. It's too much for senior citizens."

"I was looking at Rog and Geordan. They were practically shoulder to shoulder, and I heard both of them call for it," says Stringer. "As Geordan caught it and ran in across me I looked at the clock and saw the time was highlighted in red. We were roaring 'it's over, it's over'. That was a pretty good feeling. It's an extra beat of the heart, an adrenaline rush, a happiness, a great excitement. You know the hard work has paid off. That first realisation you've won a game and you've won a Grand Slam. You begin to calm down and just enjoy it. It's hard to describe it."

"Class," says Flannery - he ran to Marcus Horan - of the moment. "It's a really good affirmation of all the hard work you've done after all the gnawing doubts. They're just gone for the 12 hours or whatever after the game. You feel good for your mates who've worked so hard, and particularly where we came from. I don't think we'll fall in love with ourselves or anything. I don't think that (level of performance) would be good enough to win a Grand Slam next year. It's like Munster in 2006 but I think we've got to evolve again."

"I ran to somebody, I can't remember who," says D'Arcy. "Then I stopped, put my hands in the air. I cried, then I laughed. The next ten minutes are a bit of a blur. I remember sitting down on the floor with Heaslip, that's about it."

"I remember Drico and myself had a big hug," says Stringer. "The next thing Tomás came off the bench and lifted me up. A good oul' moment there. I remember looking at pockets of supporters going absolutely mental, and a good few behind each of the posts. The contrast between all the red sitting down and all the green going berserk. Yeah, some pretty good moments. It was much more than I expected it to be, and as each day goes by you find another bit of history. I didn't really expect to feel the way I do about it."

Kiss and the other coaches came onto the pitch, the defensive coach embracing the press officer Karl Richardson, and then the players in turn. "With the emotional outpouring at that time, there's really some special, intimate moments there and that's what it's all about. It's like an exclamation mark at the end, not a question mark or a full stop. It was a very, very satisfying achievement."

GOLDEN BOYS

At last, the so-called golden generation had reached a Holy Grail of sorts.

"It's a massive moment," said O'Connell, employing one of his favourite words. "I think I've been playing for Ireland for seven years and we've had so many close calls. It's been too long coming and we wanted this more than anything." "We've not played well the last three games but we just got the job done and got what we wanted. I wouldn't say it was a case of now or never (for this group) but it was going to be one of our best chances and it doesn't happen very often. We were lucky enough to take it."

A certain brew don't do rugby days but if they did, then that Saturday would have been it, and what topped it off perfectly for Frank O'Driscoll was that President Mary McAleese was there to present the Six Nations trophy to his son.

"It said so much for the lady. I think she's an incredible woman. You could see she loved her sport. She was the President, but yet she was like a mammy to the players. And she was in high glee."

The trophy celebration was "cool", as Flannery puts it, but the lap of honour allowed them to talk to each other and soak in what they'd achieved. "I was looking to see if I could find my mum and dad in the crowd," says Flannery, "because Paulie and Hayes were saying keep an eye out for your parents. I couldn't see them but then Paulie pointed out one of my mates, Fionn, Gerry McLoughlin's son, and I tried to get into the crowd to see them by getting over the camera tracks. But one of the security men said 'you'll bust yourself if you that that'. My mum went home that night and my dad wouldn't have been out that late, but I met her the next day at the homecoming, which was cool."

D'Arcy was chuffed to bits by one banner in the crowd.

"There were a load of people from Wexford Wanderers there. 'C'mon Wexford.' I liked it when the champagne came out. Then we were running around like idiots. I was more interested in getting a bottle of champagne into my hands and spraying somebody than I was in the trophy. I managed to see my folks and get a hug from them."

A favourite memory of the day for McNaughton was "seeing the sheer delight on the players' faces, which bordered on bewilderment, at what they had just done."

TEETOTAL

As players and supporters alike danced and sang along to Rocking All Over the World, Kiss looked on and thought: "Jeez, this is special for Ireland. It will probably transcend a lot of things I've ever experienced."

"Geordie apologised for spraying champagne in my face," says the non-drinking Stringer. "I said don't worry, that's not a problem. I think he was genuinely apologising."

"After all the jubilation I made my way down behind the goal as Brian was going around with the Cup," says Frank O'Driscoll. "When he was going by I gave him a shout. As soon as he saw me he leapt across the barrier and came over, and within half a second I was squashed against the barrier by all the people. Some fella got my head in a lock and knocked off my glasses. It was like something out of a pantomime. But that was an incredible moment. I was full of pent-up emotion and all I wanted was to give him (Brian) a hug. Looking at the expression on his face I'll never forget it. It was pure, pure joy and the release of pent-up emotions."

Back in the dressingroom, the scene was riotous; a photographer endeavouring to take pictures amid the carnage. It is, as Flannery reveals, a predetermined goal of sorts.

"We often say it before games, 'just imagine sitting down in the dressingroom after the game and the feeling when you've won a game'. It's just so satisfying knowing you've given everything you can and the fulfilment you can enjoy then. You imagine that feeling after the game. Yeah, the guys were absolutely knackered but sitting there with medals around their necks."

Some music was played, with D'Arcy putting on what seems to be something of a squad favourite by attaching his iPod to the speakers in the middle of the room. It's a track by a Manchester Indie Rock band, Elbow, called: 'One Day Like This,' which probably never seemed more appropriate.

Well, anyway, it's looking like a beautiful day
So throw those curtains wide!
One day like this a year'd see me right!

"It's got a bit of a love theme but it's about a beautiful day basically," says Kiss. "It's not a rock song, it's got this lovely theme and a few violins in it."

"It's a nice mellow song, but with a little bit of rhythm in it as well," says Smal.

It remains musical choice until Paddy 'Rala' O'Reilly gradually assumes the role of DJ and fittingly Christy Moore, who had again played a private gig for the squad on the Tuesday night prior to the Scottish game, takes over. Prince William visited the dressingroom briefly before having his photograph taken with a few of the management and players. Kidney and O'Driscoll went out to fulfil television and other media obligations.

Most had their own personal cameras and/or mobile phones to take pictures with alongside the trophies. A room near the dressingrooms was set up by the Six Nations organisers for players and staff to have photographs by an official photographer taken with the trophies, either in groups or individually. The official black tie post match banquet was supposed to start at 9.0pm in the Irish team hotel which, given the trophy presentations, was always a little on the optimistic side. Everything was running late, so much that the dinner didn't start until 10.30pm.

RUNNING LATE

The players began leaving on the team coach, some stopping off for post-match interviews with written and radio media. Because of the post match traffic, as a CIE bus driver once put it to a colleague when offered a lift, it literally would have been quicker to walk.

"But that was the first time they'd all been alone together, without anyone else," says McNaughton, "and it was a special 15 minutes for people to sit down and have a chat, or walk up and down the bus and have a few jokes. Brilliant."

The O'Driscoll clan had made their way to the Hilton Hotel, where people were being refused entry.

"We just said we were Brian O'Driscoll's family and he said: 'certainly, come in.' He didn't ask for identification or anything. Most pleasant."

Inside, they'd heard that the Irish squad had arrived via the tradesman's entrance and sneaked up to their room to change for the official post match, black tie banquet. One of the hotel managers escorted them up the back stairs to the fifth floor to the Irish captain's room.

"Brian had the trophy and we'd about 15 minutes with him on our own privately which was wonderful. No interruptions, and we were all photographed with the trophy, the whole lot of us, and Amy (Huberman) as well. It was fantastic and totally private."

Word had it on the Marianne Finucane show the next morning that Frank and Geraldine drank well into the morning hours, prompting the famous comment from their son that "I can't be held responsible for my parents' actions." But, according to Frank himself, this was an urban myth. "I don't know where they got their information from, but we had a meal at about 11.30pm in the local Italian and left to go back to bed at about 12.30am. We were just too exhausted. The day had been too draining. We were absolutely exhausted."

Their daughter Julie and her family headed off to Fishguard for the 2.30am sailing back to Rosslare, which enabled them to attend the Lord Mayor's reception in the Mansion House, Dublin the next day. The banquet ended at about 12.30am or 12.45am.

"The humility and graciousness of the Welsh," stood out for Kiss, "particularly their captain (Ryan Jones). Then there was a definite need for the squad to get together in the team room. It was beautiful."

EARLY TO BED

So, rather than head into the night, most went upstairs to the team room in the hotel, had a few drinks and enjoyed each other's company. By 2.0am, D'Arcy was in bed.

"I wanted to do my best to go out but I just couldn't. I pushed it, did my best, but I was just too tired. I'm looking forward to seeing it (the game) again. I'm sure it's the hardest thing I'll ever have to describe in terms of my feelings and everything. It's too hard to explain. Some people remember different things more vividly but what's nice is that everybody can cherish their own little bits."

"You're just trying to take in what you've done," says Flannery, "and I was thinking I don't believe Deccie has won the Grand Slam in his first year, especially coming from where we were. An unbelievable turnaround. How low confidence (was) within the squad, and yet he didn't do any reinventing the wheel. The Welsh lads were sound. It's hard to really celebrate when you're so exhausted. I probably won't even appreciate it until the season is over.

"Myself, Marcus and Keith (Earls) went to St Munchin's the following Wednesday and the place went absolutely bananas. I got a text from Dave Quinlan the day before saying 'lads, get ready for the Rocky music.' When we arrived the kids were screaming and the Rocky music was playing and I thought 'what is going on here'. And then some of the teachers spoke and I've never seen or heard them speak so passionately."

"I went to bed at about 3.0am," says Smal, "and I was probably one of the early ones."

SUNDAY AM. THE WEE HOURS

Rousing the players can't have been much fun for McNaughton or 'Rala', but the squad left their hotel on time at 11.0am for a 1.0pm flight on an Aer Arann charter: greeted by an estimated 2,000 supporters in Dublin Airport, where six or seven fire ambulances with Irish flags formed a guard of honour for the players as they disembarked. Airport staff assembled to take photographs. Dublin City Council had made contact with the IRFU the previous week to make contingency plans in the event of Ireland winning the Grand Slam, so as to avert massive crowds descending on the airport, but for obvious reasons a provisional 'homecoming' had been kept hush-hush.

A police escort took the squad to the Mansion House for a reception with the Lord Mayor, after which they met some of the great and the good, before they were presented to a crowd of about 18,000 in Dawson Street for the televised homecoming.

"That was important, because it gave people an opportunity to say thank you to us," says D'Arcy.

The most relieved man in Ireland, Paddy Wallace, could afford to quip: "I thought the game needed a little more drama."

Set alongside another display of mental and physical courage by Bernard Dunne that night, Saturday March 21st, 2009 day was a wonderful antidote to the country's economic gloom, rising employment and banker scandals. Although there were no official big screens, RTE's coverage was shown in rugby clubs and even many GAA clubs around the country. This supplemented the official average audience of 945,000 people, making it the most watched programme of the year on all channels available in Ireland.

The success also probably saved jobs in the IRFU, and fittingly, if unbeknown to most, an informal dinner and party for all the squad, wives, girlfriends, families and IRFU committee and staff, had been arranged by Kidney and McNaughton in the Killiney Castle Hotel that night. "I enjoy those days. It's a pity it has to end," admits Stringer.

It would be another long but relatively intimate night, though as far as Smal is concerned, the highlight was opening his eyes on Sunday morning in his room in the Cardiff Hilton Hotel.

"I can't tell you how nice it is to wake up that next morning and know that it's in the pocket. That's a great feeling. That's a great feeling. That's probably better than going to bed and knowing you won it. Everything looks brighter, and better."

The lyrics of the *Elbow* song seem curiously apposite to bookend the moment.

Drinking in the morning sun
Blinking in the morning sun....

Well, anyway, it's looking like a beautiful day
So throw those curtains wide!
One day like this a year'd see me right!

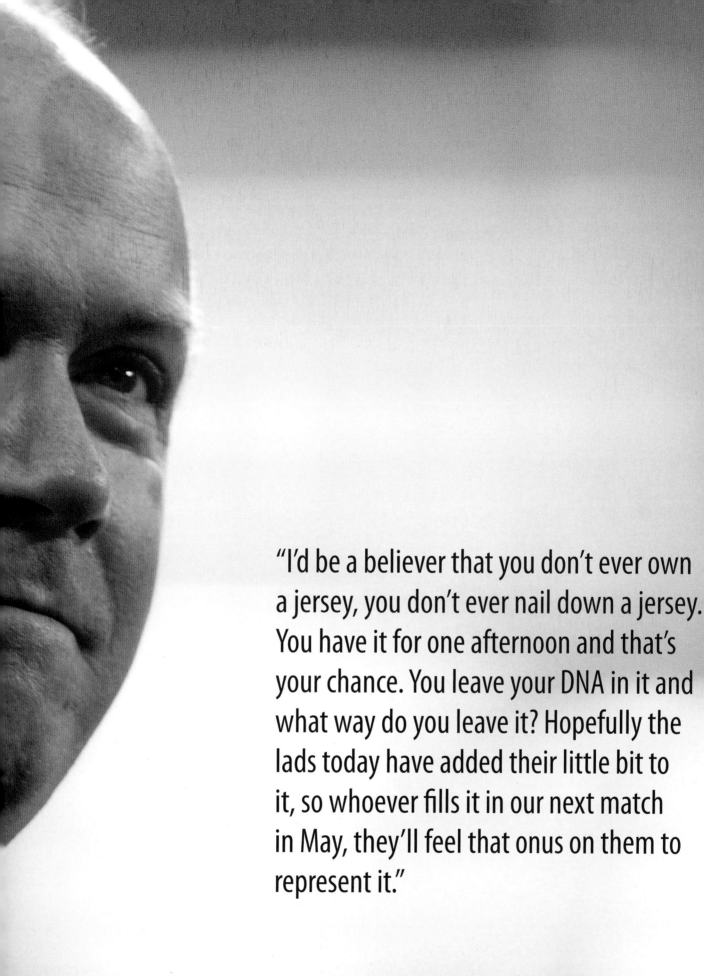

"I'd be a believer that you don't ever own a jersey, you don't ever nail down a jersey. You have it for one afternoon and that's your chance. You leave your DNA in it and what way do you leave it? Hopefully the lads today have added their little bit to it, so whoever fills it in our next match in May, they'll feel that onus on them to represent it."